New Inside Out

Ceri Jones and Jon Hird

with Russell Stannard

Advanced

Workbook

MACMILLAN

Macmillan Education
Between Towns Road, Oxford, OX4 3PP
A division of Macmillan Publishers Limited
Companies and representatives throughout the world

ISBN 978 0 2300 0933 2 (with key edition)
ISBN 978 0 2300 0934 9 (without key edition)

Original design by Jackie Hill, 320 Design Limited
Page make-up by Carolyn Gibson
Illustrated by Beach, Ray and Corrine Burroughs, Ivan Gillet, Ed McLachlan and
Nicola Slater.
Cover design by Andrew Oliver

'The Terror of Blue John Gap' by Sir Arthur Conan Doyle taken from the
Macmillan Literature Collections.
First published in the Macmillan Literature Collections, 2009.

The authors and publishers would like to thank the following for permission to reproduce
the following copyright material: HarperCollins Publishers, Dr Deborah Tannen and
Little, Brown Book Group for the synopsis taken from the back cover of *Talking from 9
to 5: Women and Men in the Workplace: Language, Sex and Power* by Deborah Tannen, New
York: Avon, 1995 copyright © Deborah Tannen. Reprinted by permission of HarperCollins
Publishers, Deborah Tannen and Little, Brown Book Group; Extract from *"Michael Holden:
All Ears"* copyright © Guardian News & Media Ltd 2007 first published in The Guardian
03.10.07, reprinted by permission of the publisher; The Random House Group Ltd for
the synopsis of *The Female Brain* by Louann Brizendine, 2008, reprinted with permission
of The Random House Group Ltd; Tammy Lenski for a simplified extract from "10 best
ways to win an argument" http://conflictzen.com/the-10-best-ways-to-win-an-argument
copyright © Tammy Lenski; Macmillan Education for extracts, pie chart and graph
adapted from *Inside Out Advanced Workbook* by Russell Stannard and Ceri Jones, copyright
© Macmillan Publishers Limited 2001, used with permission; Extract from *'In hindsight, it's
easy to scoff at past predictions'* by Robert Uhlig, copyright © Telegraph Group Limited 2000,
first published in The Daily Telegraph 31.08.00, reprinted by permission of the publisher.

These materials may contain links for third party websites. We have no control over, and
are not responsible for, the contents of such third party websites. Please use care when
accessing them.

The authors and publishers would like to thank the following for permission to reproduce
their photographic material: **Alamy**/ Imagebroker p40, Alamy/ Mihaela Ninic p45,
Alamy/ Homer W Sykes p19, Alamy/ Kathy de Witt p71; **Alma Books Ltd**/ One World
Classics Ltd p8; **Corbis**/ Heide Benser p38(t), Corbis/ Fridmarr Damm p18, Corbis/
Kevin Dodge p64, Corbis/ Michael Goulding/Orange County Register p58(r), Corbis/
Pete Leonard p38(b), Corbis/ Simon Marcus p15, Corbis/ Moodboard pp44(r), 66;
Getty/ Hulton Archives p20(b), Getty/ Popperfoto p20(t), Getty/ Purestock p59;
Photolibrary/ Morgan David de Lossy p56, Photolibrary/ Imagebroker.net p44(cr),
Photolibrary/ Photoalto p44(cl), Photolibrary/ Radius Images p38(c); **Rex Features**/
David Bolly p32, Rex Features/ Everett Collection p58(l); **Science Photo Library**/
Philippe Plailly p44(l).

Every effort has been made to trace the copyright holders, but if any have been
inadvertently overlooked the publishers will be pleased to make the necessary
arrangements at the first opportunity.

Printed and bound in Spain by Edelvives

2013   2012   2011   2010
10 9 8 7 6 5 4 3 2 1

Contents

Conversation

Grammar

1 Add the adverbials in brackets to the sentences below. Sometimes more than one position is possible.

   a) Eavesdropping can get you into big trouble! (at work)

   Eavesdropping at work can get you into big trouble!

   b) I had a really interesting conversation with a complete stranger. (recently)

   _____

   _____

   c) I hate people who talk on about themselves all the time. (endlessly)

   _____

   _____

   d) I overheard the most incredible conversation the other day! (on the bus)

   _____

   _____

   e) I speak to my grandmother on the phone. (at least once a month)

   _____

   _____

   f) I tried to phone my boyfriend, but he wasn't answering the phone. (last night)

   _____

   _____

2 Add adverbials to the following sentences so that they are true for you.

   a) I love people who speak to me. (add an adverbial saying how)

   _____

   _____

   b) I meet up with my friends to relax and have a chat. (add adverbials saying how often and where)

   _____

   _____

   c) I had a really long chat with my best friend. (add an adverbial saying when)

   _____

   _____

3 Rewrite the sentences below, changing the position of the adverbial in bold so that the meaning of the sentence changes.

   1 a) I had really wanted my parents to meet my boyfriend **earlier on in the day**.

      b) *Earlier on in the day, I had really wanted my parents to meet my boyfriend.*

   2 a) **Frankly**, she just didn't answer the question.

      b) _____

      _____

   3 a) I really regretted having asked Jane to come to the party **later**.

      b) _____

      _____

      _____

   4 a) I'd just talk to him about it **normally**.

      b) _____

   5 a) **Only** Jack knew how to read Arabic.

      b) _____

      _____

   6 a) I think she **sometimes** finds my obsession with tidiness annoying.

      b) _____

      _____

      _____

4 Match the sentences below to the correct sentence, a or b, in each pair in Exercise 3.

   1 But by the end of the afternoon, I had changed my mind. I knew it would be a huge mistake! `b`

   2 It would have been much better if she'd told the truth. ☐

   3 But by then it was too late. The invitations had been sent and there was nothing I could do about it. ☐

   4 There's no need to get angry. ☐

   5 Unfortunately he didn't know how to speak it. ☐

   6 Only sometimes? I think it annoys her pretty much all the time! ☐

5 Underline the correct form of the verb.

Well, I (1) <u>was standing</u> / **had stood** in a queue at the check out in the supermarket the other day when I overheard a really interesting conversation. One woman (2) **was telling** / **had told** another about her boyfriend. She (3) **was going** / **had gone** on and on about how wonderful he was. How he (4) **was always looking** / **had always looked** after her, cooking and cleaning and buying romantic presents. I (5) **was beginning** / **have been beginning** to feel quite jealous, when suddenly the woman's phone rang. 'Yes darling,' she answered. 'No darling, of course, darling, straight away. Yes, I (6) **'ve bought** / **'d been buying** some beer … yes, I (7) **'ve remembered** / **'m remembering** your sports magazine … no, of course I don't mind if Ben and Dan come over …. Yes, yes, I (8) **'ll be getting** / **'ll have got** the food ready while you (9) **'re watching** / **'ve watched** the football …. No, no, don't worry, you take it easy.' 'As always,' she added under her breath as she rang off. Of course, everyone else (10) **had been listening** / **had listened** too, and at that point we all looked away, trying desperately to look like we (11) **hadn't heard** / **weren't hearing** a word and (12) **were just getting** / **had just got** on with our shopping.

SPICES

DESSERTS

🌐 01 Listen and check.

6 There are mistakes in five of the sentences below. Find them and correct them. Tick the correct sentences.

a) Who would have thought he could do such a thing? He's always ~~been being~~ such a quiet person.

   *been*_____

b) This time next week I'll have laid on a golden beach, far away from everything.

   _____

c) By the time I'm 50, I'll have done everything I want to do and I'll be ready to retire.

   _____

d) If I had been born in a different country, I might be having a completely different childhood.

   _____

e) I had been standing at the bus stop waiting for a bus, when the strangest thing happened.

   _____

f) I've never really been understanding why some people don't enjoy travelling abroad.

   _____

g) He's been working on this project for such a long time, I'm glad he finally gets some recognition for it.

   _____

h) The neighbours must have been having a party last night. The noise from their flat was deafening!

   _____

7 Complete the sentences so that they are true for you. Use perfect, continuous or perfect continuous verbs where possible.

a) This time next week, I _____
   _____
   _____

b) By the time I'm 50, I _____
   _____
   _____

c) I'd been standing _____ ,
   when _____
   _____

d) I've always wanted to know why _____
   _____
   _____

e) My life might have been very different if
   _____
   _____

f) I've spent a long time trying to _____
   _____
   but _____

Vocabulary

1 **Complete the sentences with the adjectives in the box.**

~~animated~~	bizarre	frustrating	hilarious
in-depth	intense	intimate	lengthy
one-sided	pointless		

a) The discussion was really ___animated___ , with voices raised and people shouting, but in excitement, not in anger.

b) His opening speech was _____ . We haven't laughed so much for a long time.

c) It was so _____ trying to explain the problem to him. I didn't know what else to say to make him understand.

d) The discussion we had on the future of the company was _____ and well-researched and we felt that we'd made some progress.

e) I thought the meeting was _____ . The management team clearly had no intention of listening to our arguments.

f) It was a _____ conversation but in the end we did manage to come to an agreement.

g) I got caught up in this totally _____ conversation with a complete stranger. I swear I have no idea what she was talking about!

h) Conversations with Elizabeth are always so _____ . She never lets anyone else get a word in edgeways!

i) They were sat at a table for two, oblivious of all around them and engaged in an _____ and _____ conversation.

2 **Replace the words in bold with a verb or expression from the box in the correct form.**

always have something to say	butt in
be on the same wavelength	drone on and on
flow	hog	hunt around for	~~put across~~

a) It was really difficult to **convey** the underlying concept. ___put across___

b) We get on really well together. We seem to **share similar views and values**. _____

c) The conversation **was really easy and comfortable** and the time flew. _____

d) Excuse me, I hope you don't mind me **interrupting** like this. _____

e) His lectures are so boring, he just **talks and talks** in a monotone voice. _____

f) I don't enjoy talking to Rod. He always **dominates** the conversation and never listens to what other people have to say. _____

g) There was a long, embarrassing silence and I was forced to **think of** a new topic to bring the conversation back to life! _____

h) Jude is really interesting. He **is never at a loss for words**, no matter who he's talking to. _____

3 **Complete the sentences with words and expressions from Exercise 2.**

a) Kris is so rude. He's forever ___butting in___ to other people's conversations.

b) Sorry! Have I been _____ the conversation? I'd better shut up and let someone else have a turn!

c) I love talking to Brett. He's so funny, and the conversation really _____ . You never have to _____ things to say.

d) She's really got a way with words. She always knows how to _____ her point _____ , and how to bring people round to her point of view.

e) I wish Kath would shut up sometimes. She just _____ about the same things all the time.

f) They're very much in love! They clicked from the first meeting and are obviously _____ .

Do you know anyone like the people described above? If so, write a sentence about them.

4 Underline the correct word.

a) The ability to be tactful is a great <u>skill</u> / skilled / skilfulness.

b) She works so **efficient / efficiency / efficiently** with her new computer that she gets the job done in half the time.

c) He's completely lacking in **competence / competent / competently** and can't do the job properly.

d) I'm looking for a job where I can **fulfilment / fulfil / fulfilling** my ambition to write.

e) It's very **satisfaction / satisfying / satisfied** when people congratulate you on making a good presentation.

f) He's got no **consideration / consider / considerate** for anyone, he just does what he wants and expects everyone to fit in with him.

g) Do you think getting that report finished by five o'clock is really **achievement / achievable / unachievable**?

5 Complete the sentences with the correct form of the words in brackets.

a) She's a very ___considerate___ person and always thinks about the needs of the people around her. (consider)

b) I really don't think your work is _____ . You're going to have to make much more effort if you hope to pass the exam. (satisfy)

c) It really is one of the most _____ jobs I've done. It's great to see the students making so much progress. (fulfil)

d) Your son's worked hard this term and should feel very proud of his _____ . (achieve)

e) The shortage of _____ workers is a big problem at the moment. (skill)

f) That's not a very _____ way of working. I'm sure you could do the job much faster. (efficiency)

g) He's a very _____ driver. He'll have no problem passing his test. (competence)

6 Complete the conversation openers. The first letter of each missing word is given for you.

a) *Fancy*_____ meeting you here! Are you at the conference?

b) What a s_____ ! I wasn't e_____ to see you here!

c) Hi, you m_____ be Rhona. I've h_____ a lot about you.

d) Excuse me, have you g_____ a pen I could borrow?

e) Hi! How are t_____ with you?

f) Wow! This is a g_____ place!

7 Write the words in the correct order. Add commas where necessary.

1 hope good All I !
   All good, I hope!

2 sec. a Just Here Yes have. are. I you
   _____

3 all. bad Not at you about what And ?
   _____

4 first Yes days. am I for the two you And ?
   _____

5 Likewise! Lottie knew you had I idea no .
   _____

6 know it's I amazing totally !
   _____

8 🌐 02 Match the openers in Exercise 6 with the replies above. Then listen and check.

a	b	c	d	e	f
4					

Pronunciation

1 Add question tags to the sentences.

a) You'll be there, *won't you* ?

b) He's done this before, _____ ?

c) We might be going again next week, _____ ?

d) You've forgotten to switch the gas off, _____ ?

e) I couldn't allow her to pay for herself, _____ ?

f) He won't let it happen again, _____ ?

2 🌐 03 Listen to the first sentence being said twice and answer the questions.

1 In which sentence, 1 or 2, does the speaker's voice rise, ☐ and in which does it fall? ☐

2 In which sentence, 1 or 2, is the speaker
   a) confirming something they already know? ☐
   b) asking for confirmation from someone? ☐

3 🌐 04 Listen to the sentences from Exercise 1 again, with their tags. Decide if the intonation on each tag question rises (↗) or falls (↘). Listen again and repeat.

a	b	c	d	e	f
↗					

Reading

Books of the week

ALL EaRS
michael HOLDEN
illustrated by
andy watt

"Alan Bennett meets Samuel Beckett for a slacker generation."
— The Observer

A *All Ears*
by Michael Holden

As the author of *All Ears* will freely admit, there's nothing dignified about listening to other people's conversations, especially if these are thrust upon us as we stand on a crowded London bus, packed sardine-style with complete strangers shouting into their mobile phones. No one, however, has ever attempted to raise eavesdropping to an art form, or recognize what verbal gems are being thrown around us every minute of our waking urban existence. Gathered for the first time in a volume, and accompanied by Andy Watt's iconic illustrations, are Michael Holden's hit "stolen dialogues". The locations vary — ranging from Scotland to the South Coast — but the focus is on the teeming city of London, with its noisy and multifarious inhabitants, directly presented here in all its quirkiness, showing how unusual and unscriptable everyday conversation can at times be. The book includes fifteen colour illustrations by Andy Watt and scene-setting descriptions for each dialogue.

B *Talking from 9 to 5*
by Deborah Tannen

In her extraordinary international bestseller, *You Just Don't Understand*, Deborah Tannen transformed forever the way we look at intimate relationships between women and men. Now she turns her keen ear and observant eye toward the workplace — where the ways in which men and women communicate can determine who gets heard, who gets ahead, and what gets done.

An instant classic, *Talking From 9 to 5* brilliantly explains women's and men's conversational rituals — and the language barriers we unintentionally erect in the business world. It is a unique and invaluable guide to recognizing the verbal power games and miscommunications that cause good work to be underappreciated or go unnoticed — an essential tool for promoting more positive and productive professional relationships among men and women.

C *The Female Brain*
by Louann Brizendine

While conducting research as a medical student at Yale and then as a resident and faculty member at Harvard, Louann Brizendine discovered that almost all of the clinical data in existence on neurology and psychology focused exclusively on males. In response to this, Brizendine established the first clinic in the US to study and treat women's brains. At the same time, America's National Institute of Health began to regularly include female subjects in its studies for the first time. The combined result has been an explosion of new data on the female brain.

Exploring many of the questions relating to the differences between the way men and women think and behave — questions which have stumped the scientists throughout the ages — this revolutionary book combines two decades of Brizendine's own work, real life stories from her clinical practice, and all of the latest information from the scientific community at large to provide a truly comprehensive look at the way women's minds work. Fun, accessible and often surprising, this is a unique 'owner's manual' for women!

1 🌐 05 **Read the book reviews and match each book to one of the brief descriptions below.**

a) a book about how women's minds work

b) a humorous book about overheard conversations

c) a book about the differences between men and women at work

2 Read the reviews again. Which book ...

a) was written by a trained doctor?

b) was first published as a series of articles?

c) is based on years of clinical research?

d) is not the first book the author has written on a similar topic?

e) reports day-to-day conversations?

f) concentrates on communication problems?

g) claims to be exploring a new area of research?

h) has pictures in it?

3 Do you think the reviews have been written by

a) professional book critics?

b) the publishers?

4 Look at the reviews again and find words that mean:

a) very tightly, without being able to move (review A) _____

b) very busy and full of people (review A) _____

c) varied (review A) _____

d) succeeds (review B) _____

e) put up (review B) _____

f) puzzled (review C) _____

g) easy to understand and enjoy (review C) _____

Writing

1 Read the article and decide if these statements are true (*T*) or false (*F*).

The writer …

a) is giving advice about how to win an argument.

b) is giving advice about how to avoid an argument.

c) is trying to amuse the readers.

d) has a serious message to put across.

5 sure steps to winning an argument

The next time you have an argument with a loved one, use these five simple steps, and you're sure to come out on top.

1 Scream, shout, sob loudly, or go deadly silent. Whatever way you show anger, just be sure to do it thoroughly and with great drama. The more histrionics the better.

2 Use the words *always* and *never*. You're *always* starting arguments. You *never* help with the housework. This strategy's a good one because your opponent will get sidetracked as they try to defend themselves against your accusations.

3 Blame the other person for the argument. They started it, after all, by doing X, Y or Z. Or by being born. Things like this are never your fault. You are simply an innocent victim of their problem and it's important that they know that. Again.

4 Remind them you're right, they're wrong. And not just 50%,of the time, but the whole 100%. You, of course, are always right, particularly when you're angry.

5 Between arguments, make up, but only on the surface. Don't waste time in the kind of conversation that will help heal the damage to your relationship. Don't really talk things out and get to the heart of the matter. Otherwise, how are you going to win the next argument?

Follow these five easy steps and you're sure to have a life full of long, hard arguments. However, if you're looking for a bit of peace and quiet, try doing the opposite, and, who knows, you might find yourself in a harmonious, loving relationship.

2 Look at the extracts from the article. What do the words in bold refer to?

a) Whatever way you show anger, just be sure to do **it** thoroughly and with great drama.

b) **This** strategy's a good one because your opponent will get sidetracked

c) They started **it**, after all, by doing X, Y or Z.

d) You are simply an innocent victim of **their** problem.

e) Don't really talk things out and get to the heart of **the matter**.

f) If you're looking for a bit of peace and quiet, try doing **the opposite.**

3 Complete this tip with one word in each gap.

> **Refuse to apologize.**
>
> Tell yourself, (1) _____ were awful too, so *they* should have to reach out to *you* first. Tell yourself (2) _____ again. The more you tell yourself (3) _____ story, the more justified you will feel in refusing to admit you contributed to (4) _____ mess.

4 Look at the article again. Find …

a) three affirmative imperative forms

_____

b) two negative imperative forms

_____

c) a rhetorical question

_____

d) a conditional sentence

_____

5 Does the article …

a) talk directly to the reader?

b) talk about the problem in an abstract way?

6 Write a tip sheet with the title '5 sure steps to avoiding an argument'. Look at the tips below. Which would you like to include? Can you think of any others? When you've chosen your five tips, write short notes on each one.

- Always take the blame
- Be ready to say you're sorry
- Don't raise your voice
- Listen to what they have to say
- Stay calm
- Never accuse a person of being wrong
- Explain your side of the story in detail
- Be sympathetic
- Try to make a joke

7 Now write your tip sheet. Use about 250 words. Use a simple, straightforward style.

2 Taste

Grammar

1 Underline all the noun phrases in this text which have three words or more.

We had <u>a great dinner</u>. Lucy cooked for us, she's a fantastic cook. We started with these gorgeous little smoked salmon pancakes. They were absolutely delicious! Then we had some cold cucumber soup and tiny little fingers of crisp toast. The main course was incredible, you really should have seen it. She brought out a tray of fresh lobsters and served them up with a very simple green salad. I thought I couldn't possibly eat any more, but when she brought out the dessert, a home-made chocolate mousse, it was just too good to resist!

2 Reorder these words and phrases to form complex noun phrases that describe different types of drink.

a) wine / with just a hint of vanilla / delicate / white / sweet / a

a delicate sweet white wine with just a hint of vanilla

b) piping hot / straight from the pot / tea / a cup of / lovely

_____

_____

c) citrus / a mixture of / with just a touch of champagne / juices / tangy

_____

_____

d) and a slice of lemon / water / with a couple of fresh mint leaves / ice cold / a glass of

_____

_____

e) full-fat / straight from the fridge / a glass of / milk /fresh

_____

_____

f) hot / on top / a steaming cup of / with a dollop of cream / chocolate

_____

_____

3 Write the words in italics in the correct order.

a) a tub of vanilla ice cream with *chocolate dark delicious* flakes.

delicious dark chocolate

b) a bowl of *bean Mexican spicy* soup

_____

c) the smell of *black Italian strong* coffee

_____

d) her *ceramic exquisite hand-painted* bowl

_____

e) a *large red shiny* apple

_____

f) half a dozen *blue speckled tiny* quail's eggs

_____

g) a *china new beautiful* tea set

_____

h) a glass of the *French ice-cold best* champagne

_____

4 Write detailed descriptions of the following things. Use at least three adjectives each time.

a) something you ate for breakfast today

_____

b) a typical regional dish from your town

_____

c) the last thing you had to drink

_____

d) your favourite comfort food

_____

e) a kind of food you really don't enjoy

_____

f) the dish you most enjoy cooking

_____

g) something your mother cooks

_____

5 Find two examples of fronting in each of the three texts below. Then rewrite them in a more informal style.

a WITH FIVE MINUTES left it was still 0–0 and everything to play for. One of the Liverpool players went in with a hard tackle and down went Chelsea's star player, Luca Romano, but not for long. Jumping to his feet, Luca got the ball, slipped past the last defender and kicked the ball as hard as he could. In went the ball and the crowd went mad. Chelsea 1 – Liverpool 0.

1 _Chelsea's star player Luca Romano went down_
2 _____
  _____

b Gone are the days when the boss played God over an office of cowering underlings. Equality is the name of the game in business today, with everyone taking an equal share of the work and, likewise, an equal share of the responsibility, or at least that's what the gurus would have us believe.

1 _____
  _____
2 _____
  _____

c The centre of the old medieval town had been devastated. In the main square stood the cathedral, it's dome cracked and crumbling. The narrow streets, once shady, quiet retreats from the summer sun, were now full of rubble. Through the broken facades could be glimpsed the personal and private worlds of the people who lost their homes, their loved ones, their lives.

1 _____
  _____
2 _____
  _____

6 Rewrite the sentences fronting the words in bold.

a) The rain came **down** and washed the dust away.
   Down came the rain and washed the dust away.

b) The sound of raised voices could be heard **in the kitchen**.
   _____

c) Half a dozen fishing boats were **bobbing** gently on the water.
   _____

d) The name of the restaurant was **The Western Isle.**
   _____

e) The best words to describe it are **homely,** simple and down-to-earth.
   _____

f) The days of peace and harmony were **long** gone.
   _____

g) We didn't really know **what** had happened.
   _____

h) We had no idea **when** she'd be coming back.
   _____

Pronunciation

Look at the words in the box. Write them alongside the appropriate stress pattern. The first one has been done for you.

| ~~cauliflower~~ convenience   criticism   cucumber |
| delicious   exquisite   intricate   microwave |
| refreshing   selection   strawberries   vegetables |

a) ■ ■ ■ ■ _cauliflower_ _____

b) ■ ■ ■ _____

c) ■ ■ ■ _____
   _____

🔊 06 Listen and check.

Vocabulary

1 Complete the sentences with the words in the box. You may need to make some changes to the verbs.

> bob   chug   clientele   concrete   launch
> reverie   satnav   ~~thriving~~   thrust

a) What had once been a ___thriving___ fishing community was now just a collection of abandoned cottages.

b) She looked up from her _____ to see that the platform had cleared and her train had gone.

c) The restaurant had a very cosmopolitan _____ and a lively atmosphere.

d) He punched the address into the _____ , sat back in the driver's seat and thought of the journey ahead.

e) They looked in dismay at the petrol gauge as the car _____ slowly to a halt at the side of the road.

f) The man walked up to me, _____ a letter into my hand and then rushed away.

g) The village was very quiet and picturesque with the small fishing boats _____ gently in the small stone harbour.

h) The old hotel had been replaced by an ugly _____ monstrosity that towered over the houses nearby.

i) He sped to the side of the jetty in his new _____ , looking very pleased with himself.

2 Replace a word or phrase in each sentence with a word or phrase from the box.

> batter   blared out   clientele   entrepreneur
> exquisite   ~~homely~~   pricey   reverie
> sped off   thriving

a) It's a simple, comfortable and ~~informal~~ restaurant run by a family. ___homely___

b) The food was fantastic – perfectly cooked and beautifully presented. _____

c) Our meal was spoilt by the music which played loudly from a loudspeaker above our table. _____

d) That restaurant's far too expensive. Let's find somewhere else to eat. _____

e) He runs a successful restaurant just outside Rome. _____

f) The fish was coated in a mixture of flour, milk and egg whites, and then deep fried. _____

g) The new company was set up by a businessman with plenty of money and new ideas. _____

h) The restaurant's regular customers come from far and wide. _____

i) We jumped in the car and drove away quickly. _____

j) A loud knock interrupted my daydream. _____

3 Match the sentence beginnings (*a–f*) with their endings (*1–6*).

a) I think he's got great taste in clothes,
b) I think that joke was in very bad taste,
c) It's a place with something for all tastes,
d) Fresh fruit from Spain has so much taste,
e) The main course was very tasty but
f) I'm not quite sure about the taste,

1 it's a joy to go shopping at the markets there.
2 it was offensive and certainly not funny.
3 perhaps it needs a bit more garlic.
4 he always looks so smart and elegant.
5 where all the family will find something to do.
6 I was disappointed with the dessert.

a	b	c	d	e	f
4					

4 Complete the sentences with words formed from *taste*.

a) Our meal in that new restaurant was dreadful. The food was completely __*tasteless*__ .

b) The choice of colours was very _____ . It was obvious that whoever owned the house had a good eye for colours.

c) She works as a chocolate _____ for a supermarket chain.

d) The beer festival normally starts quite seriously, with everyone _____ the different beers on offer and commenting on them.

e) I thought the whole wedding ceremony was _____ . I mean who in their right mind would have a priest dressed as Elvis Presley?

f) That really was a _____ meal. I must remember to come here again.

g) She was clearly a very elegant woman. She was _____ dressed in a grey jacket and black trousers.

5 Use one word to complete the sentences. The first letter has been given to help you.

a) We both apologised to each other later, but the incident left a b*ad*_____ taste in my mouth.

b) *Black olives* are definitely an a_____ taste. I didn't like them as a child, but I love them now.

c) I get on really well with my *new flatmate*. We s_____ the same taste in everything!

d) I don't understand people who *listen to rock music first thing in the morning*. But I suppose there's no a_____ for taste!

e) I used to complain about the service in restaurants. Now I'm working as a waiter and I'm getting a taste of my own m_____ .

f) The home team scored a goal in the last minute to taste v_____ for the first time in their new stadium.

g) The joke was in very p_____ taste and no-one laughed.

6 Look at b–d in Exercise 5 again. Replace the words in italics to make these sentences true for you.

b) _____

c) _____

d) _____

7 Underline the best alternative in conversations a–d.

a)

Ruby: Have you heard? Jo's thinking of leaving her job.

Tom: (1) **I suppose you're right. / That can't be right!** I was talking to her the other night and she seemed really happy with her job.

Ruby: (2) **That may be, but / I know, it's awful,** she told me that she and Greg are going to open a restaurant.

b)

Tom: We went to Jo and Greg's new restaurant last night.

Ruby: And?

Tom: Well, I hate to say it, but the service was really slow and the food was terrible!

Ruby: (3) **I rest my case. / I know, it's awful, isn't it?** We went a couple of nights ago and I was really embarrassed for them.

c)

Jo: The customers have been complaining about the service again. They say it's really slow.

Greg: But (4) **that's a load of rubbish! / I suppose you're right!** We're all working as quickly as we can and no-one's had to wait more than about ten minutes.

Jo: Well, (5) **I think you'll find that / that may be, but** the couple in the corner have been waiting for more than half an hour.

d)

Jack: This is one of the worst restaurants I've ever been to!

Ella: (6) **Oh, I don't know, / I suppose you're right,** the staff are friendly and the décor's nice ... Ah, here's the fish ... Oh, no, it's cold!

Jack: And it's only half-cooked! (7) **That's a load of rubbish! / I rest my case!**

Ella: (8) **I suppose you're right. / No way!**

🌐 **07 Listen and check.**

Listening

1   ⊕ 08 **Cover the script opposite and listen to four stories about people's experiences in restaurants. Then choose an appropriate title for each one.**

a) Open all hours

b) A quiet night out?

c) A fishy tale

d) A free lunch

story	1	2	3	4
title				

2   **Listen again. In which story is there:**

a) a case of mistaken identity?

b) an illness?

c) a violent incident?

d) a generous gesture?

story	1	2	3	4
topic				

3   **Which stories might these sentences come from?**

a) It's great to see you. You know, Luis was asking after you. He was wondering if you were still working on that translation project. ☐

b) Don't worry. I eat here all the time. Let me do the ordering. ☐

c) I've had enough of this! I'm not going to stand for it any longer! ☐

d) There's plenty of wine behind the bar and the music is by the stereo. ☐

4   **Complete the sentences with the words in the box. You will need to use some of them more than once.**

> at   on   to   up

a) He insisted _____ ordering.

b) I'm allergic _____ shellfish.

c) I noticed a couple waving _____ me.

d) He put _____ a special night for us.

e) As the evening went _____ , we all started dancing.

f) At twelve o'clock Petros came _____ to me.

g) He asked us to lock everything _____ when we left.

h) He started shouting _____ the waiter.

i) He ended _____ with his face in my soup.

Check your answers in the script.

1   On our first date, my boyfriend took me to a really posh restaurant. Clearly wanting to impress me, he insisted on ordering, so I said fine, but warned him not to order anything with shellfish in it – I'm allergic to it. I thought I'd made myself perfectly clear about this and that he knew what he was ordering, but obviously he didn't. An hour later I was in an ambulance being rushed to hospital. I could hardly breathe. My boyfriend looked rather embarrassed sitting by my side holding the oxygen mask to my face.

2   I was in a restaurant with my wife one evening and I couldn't help noticing a couple waving to me from a different table. Eventually the man came over, said hello and started talking about something I knew nothing about. He then said, 'Goodbye, Pablo' and sat back down at his table. We finished our meal and asked for the bill. The waiter told us that the man on the other table, who'd since left, had paid it for us. I'm absolutely certain I'd never met him in my life.

3   I used to live in a little village in Crete, and each Friday my friends and I would go down to the port to eat at our favourite restaurant. The owner, Petros, was a lovely guy and when I told him my friend was coming over from England, he said he'd put on a special night for us. And he certainly did. It was amazing, the food was out of this world. As the evening went on, we all started dancing, and when it got to twelve o'clock, Petros came up to me. I thought he was going to ask us to leave, but instead he gave me the keys to the restaurant and told me we could stay as long as we liked providing we didn't forget to lock everything up!

4   We were sitting in a restaurant in Manchester when we noticed three guys on the next table who were obviously getting frustrated because the service was so slow. Suddenly one of them stood up and started shouting at the waiter and telling him to hurry up with his food. The waiter answered back rather rudely and the next minute everything went ballistic. One of the guys ran into the kitchen and started a fight with a chef and the other two began fighting with the waiters. It was like something out of a cowboy film, with bodies flying everywhere! Finally, one of the chefs came flying across our table and ended up with his face in my soup. The crazy thing is, they still made us pay the bill and we weren't even offered a discount.

Writing

Writing a letter of complaint
Paragraph organisation

1 Read the review below for a restaurant that has just opened. Then answer these questions:

a) What kind of food does it serve?

b) What is the atmosphere like?

c) Is it expensive?

Restaurant of the week

IF YOU HAVEN'T been to Casa Paco yet, then you don't know what you're missing. This cosy little tapas bar has just opened on the High Street. It is set out like a farmhouse kitchen, with simple pine furniture, traditional Spanish earthenware and a huge fire blazing in the grate. The atmosphere is laid-back and friendly, and the clientele a mixture of students, young professionals and friends of the Spanish couple who run the place. The menu offers an incredibly wide selection of dishes, ranging from classic tortillas to the exquisite daily specials conjured up on the spot by Paco and his wife Laura. The quality of the food is superb, a difficult task with such an amazing range of delicacies to prepare. We tried more than fifteen dishes between us, each one better than the last. The shellfish is so fresh you can still smell the sea, the meat succulent and done to a turn, the sweets quite something to behold. It can get quite busy at the weekend, but the staff are never flustered and it's always service with a smile. Perhaps the secret lies in the smooth Latin sounds playing softly in the background. All this for the price of your average pizza. If you're looking for a new eating experience, head for Casa Paco. You won't be disappointed!

2 You were so impressed by the review that you decided to book a table at Casa Paco for a surprise birthday party for a very close friend. The evening was a total disaster. Look at the list below and choose four or five of the problems to describe your evening.

- half the dishes on the menu were unavailable
- the waiters were surly
- the service was incredibly slow
- the restaurant was packed
- you had to wait half an hour for your table
- you were expected to share a table with another group of people
- some of the dishes were cold by the time they arrived on the table
- it was very expensive – definitely over-priced!

3 You are going to write a letter of complaint to the magazine the review appeared in. Before you do, read a letter written by another angry reader, complaining about a recent review printed in the same magazine and answer these questions.

a) What was the review for?

b) Why is the writer of the letter so angry?

Dear Editor,

Having recently read a rave review in your magazine for the latest John Howard film, I immediately phoned my local cinema and booked three tickets for myself and two friends. We were looking forward to a great evening, but I'm sad to say that we were grievously disappointed.

Your reviewer had described the film as a 'fun-packed adventure story' and we had gone in the hope of taking our minds off the stresses and strains of a hard week at work. It turned out that the film was far from light-hearted. The plot was depressing – the story of a young man fighting a life-threatening disease, the film itself long and very slow-moving and the ending one of the saddest I've ever seen at the cinema. In brief, the review was totally misleading. The film itself is very good, but I would only recommend it for those looking for a real tear-jerker.

I'm sorry to say that after such an awful experience I don't think I'll ever be able to trust your reviews again. I suggest you take more care in the future or you will lose more loyal readers like myself.

Yours disappointedly,
Rob Walters

4 In which paragraph is the writer

a) referring to the future?

b) contrasting the film and the review?

c) explaining the reason for writing the letter?

5 Follow the paragraph structure in the model letter above and write your own letter of complaint to the magazine about their restaurant review. Read the letter again and underline any useful language that you think you could use in your letter. You should write about 200 words.

3 City

Grammar

1 Underline seven examples of hedging in the text below. The first one has been done for you.

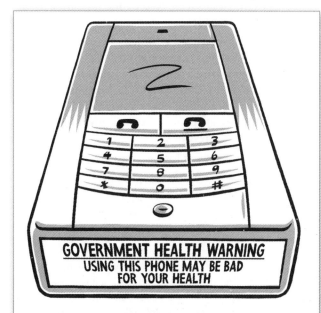

GOVERNMENT HEALTH WARNING
USING THIS PHONE MAY BE BAD
FOR YOUR HEALTH

Are mobile phones the new cigarettes?

It has been suggested that cellular phones will be the tobacco of the 21st century. It appears that their use is almost as addictive as cigarettes, with psychologists' reports claiming that there is evidence that users display withdrawal symptoms if deprived of their mobiles for more than 24 hours. There is certainly no doubt that mobile phone use in public is just as annoying as smoking. Mobile-free zones are already being set up in cinemas and restaurants, and it would seem that trains will soon be following suit, with 'mobile' and 'non-mobile' carriages available on all the commuter services to London. On a more serious note, it is now widely believed that excessive mobile phone use may cause cancer, and it has been proposed that all mobile phones should carry a government health warning similar to the one displayed on cigarette packets.

2 Complete the sentences by choosing two possible answers from the box.

appear	~~appears~~	believed	evidence
hardly any	little	proof	proved
recognised	seem	~~seems~~	shown

a) It ___*appears*___ / ___*seems*___ that the population of many modern industrialised cities is beginning to decline.

b) There is _____ / _____ doubt that in the future we will have to take radical action to control traffic congestion in our cities.

c) It is generally _____ / _____ that living in cities with a population of over a million people can be detrimental to our health.

d) There is little _____ / _____ that the levels of toxic pollution in the major cities in the U.S. are beginning to decline.

e) It would _____ / _____ that the changes in weather patterns could endanger large urban populations in low-lying land areas due to the rise in the sea level.

f) It has been _____ / _____ that prolonged exposure to the sun can cause skin cancer.

3 Rewrite these sentences using the words in brackets.

a) Smoking can lead to cancer. (no doubt)
   There is no doubt that smoking can lead to cancer.

b) Scientists in many countries believe that climate change is the greatest challenge facing our society. (widely) _____
   _____
   _____

c) There is evidence to suggest that the rate of population growth in China is beginning to decrease. (appears) _____
   _____

d) There is a general feeling that people believe governments are not doing enough about global warming. (would seem)
   _____
   _____
   _____

4 Complete the negative and limiting adverbial phrases in the sentences below using *no, not* or *only*.

   a) The teacher told them that on __*no*__ account were they to leave the school premises.

   b) _____ after a long wait did we finally get to hear the results of the tests.

   c) We were told that under _____ circumstances were we to use our mobile phones.

   d) _____ even in summer are there so many tourists to be seen in the town.

   e) _____ until he'd left university did he really appreciate how much he'd enjoyed being a student.

   f) In _____ other world capital will you find the same incredible mix of nationalities.

   g) _____ once in the whole time I knew him did he ever make a mistake in judgement.

   h) _____ after spending a few months here will you understand how this city survives.

5 Complete the adverbial phrases with the words in the box.

   | ~~after~~ | after | barely | never | only |
   | rarely | seldom | sooner | | |

   a) I realised how much I loved the city only ____*after*____ I had left it.

   b) We had no _____ moved in to our new cottage than our troubles began.

   c) The local people were not _____ rude to us, but they also ignored the children.

   d) We had _____ imagined that people could be so hostile.

   e) We made our first friend only _____ two months.

   f) We very _____ saw him, however, and life was still lonely.

   g) The children had _____ been so quiet before.

   h) We decided to go back to the city. We had _____ put up a 'For Sale' sign when the people began to be friendly towards us!

   🌐 09 Listen and check.

6 Rewrite the sentences in Exercise 5 so that they begin with the adverbial phrases you completed.

   a) *Only after I had left the city did I realise how much I loved it.*

   b) _____
      _____

   c) _____
      _____
      _____

   d) _____
      _____
      _____

   e) _____

   f) _____
      _____

   g) _____
      _____

   h) _____
      _____

Pronunciation

1 Look at the sentences below. Underline all the examples of the sound /ɔ:/.

   a) Its beauty is not as <u>awe</u>-inspiring as other cities.

   b) The streets are lined with soaring office blocks.

   c) You're constantly jostled by hawkers and hordes of tourists.

   d) The suburbs haven't fallen prey to supermarket culture.

   e) It's a living city and you'll never run out of things to explore.

   f) It's the city's hyperactive rush that really draws the people here.

   🌐 10 Listen and check.

2 Look at the words in the box. Cross out the ones that don't contain the sound /ɔ:/.

crowded	dawn	dormitory	gawp
gorge	law	modern	portray
splendour	world		

   🌐 11 Listen and check.

Vocabulary

1 **Match the adjectives *a–f* with their opposites *1–6*.**

a) haphazard	1	modest
b) tacky	2	unimpressive
c) bustling	3	organised
d) soaring	4	stylish
e) in-your-face	5	sleepy
f) awe-inspiring	6	low-rise

a	b	c	d	e	f
3					

2 **Underline the one word in each group which does not collocate with the adjective.**

a) haphazard: arrangement <u>magazine</u> system

b) tacky: clothes decorations meeting

c) bustling: family market place streets

d) soaring: houses mountain tops office blocks

e) in-your-face: celebrities chat fashions

f) awe-inspiring: performance sight village

3 **Complete the sentences with adjectives from Exercises 1 and 2.**

a) I think the plastic souvenirs some people buy on holiday are really _____*tacky*_____ .

b) With its 24-hour culture centred on gambling and entertainment, its neon signs and its brash nature, Las Vegas is one of the world's most _____ cities.

c) Arriving in Hong Kong harbour, you're immediately struck by the _____ skyscrapers that stretch as far as the eye can see.

d) The streets were _____ with people waiting for the procession to start.

e) The council planned the new one-way system in a very _____ way. I kept getting lost and having to ask for directions.

f) The first sight of Mount Kilimanjaro on a clear day is _____ .

4 **Use these adjectives to talk about something you have seen or somewhere you have been.**

stylish <u>*Our receptionist was wearing a very stylish*</u>
<u>*jacket yesterday.*</u>
_____

tacky _____
_____

awe-inspiring _____
_____

soaring _____
_____

in-your-face _____
_____

bustling _____
_____

5 **Replace the expressions in bold with the expressions in the box. Make any necessary changes to the expressions.**

> fall prey to   live on top of one another
> ~~to make way for a new~~   work its magic
> put a finger on something

a) They knocked down the old stadium **in order to put a** shopping centre **in its place.**
   <u>*to make way for a new shopping centre*</u>

b) I could never **quite understand** what he saw in her.

   _____

c) They were a family of eight and they **were all crammed in together** in a small two-bedroom flat.

   _____

d) I **became a victim of** the charms of the street vendors with their beautiful silk scarves and silver jewellery.

   _____

e) I arrived tired and stressed after an eventful journey, but as I sat at the water's edge, the view of the sun setting on the water **helped me relax.**

   _____

6 Solve the anagrams (*a–g*) and then match them to the definitions (*1–7*).

a) kesbusr _____buskers_____ _4_

b) hekcc tou _____ ____

c) rgoeg _____ ____

d) ntar _____ ____

e) pawg ta _____ ____

f) yihdnal _____ ____

g) etasreie _____ ____

1 conveniently
2 places where you can have a meal
3 a loud and protracted complaint
4 musicians who play or sing on the street
5 to go and see what something's like
6 to watch, look at or stare at someone
7 to eat an enormous amount of food

7 Complete the text with words and phrases from Exercise 6.

Covent Garden is a great place to chill out, sit back and watch the world go by. There's a whole range of different (1) ____eateries____ lining the square, serving all kinds of food from all over the world. You can choose whether you want to just pick at the bar snacks served at the street cafés, or (2) _____ yourself on the 'As much as you can eat for a tenner' buffet at the Taj Indian restaurant, (3) _____ situated just around the corner from the covered market. There are always plenty of celebrities around for you to (4) _____ , and usually one or two self-proclaimed politicians enjoying an endless (5) _____ about the state of the nation. If you prefer a spot of street theatre or a bit of music, (6) _____ the street artists and the (7) _____ . They're always guaranteed to pull a crowd.

🎧 12 **Listen and check.**

8 Add *do*, *does* or *did* to the sentences below. Change the verbs in the original sentences if necessary.

a) I really ⎰*did enjoy*⎱ ~~enjoyed~~ the film last night. It's one of the best films I've ever seen.

b) You're right about the new stadium. It looks a bit out of place.

c) Shopping malls are fine if you're looking for convenience, but I think local street markets are much more interesting.

d) Our neighbours are really friendly, but they make a lot of noise sometimes!

e) My primary school was really small, but it had an enormous playground.

f) My office is a mess. It really needs a good, thorough reorganisation.

9 Write the words in the correct order.

a) about it / I love most / The thing / is / the dome / .
The thing I love most about it is the dome.

b) the sunlight / It's / I love / that / it reflects / the way that / .
_____

c) from the tower / are / What / the spectacular views / I also like / .
_____
_____

d) you have to / is that / One thing / pay to / I don't like / go inside the cathedral / .
_____
_____

e) swaying in the wind / It's / with / the square / its palm trees / I love / that / .
_____
_____

f) is / I really like / there's always / the fact that / What / a cool sea breeze / .
_____
_____

10 Write three sentences about a place you particularly like.

a) The thing I _____
_____

b) What I _____
_____

c) It's the _____
_____

Reading

1 🌐 13 **Read the text opposite. In what ways have the Olympic Games changed since they were first reinstated in 1896?**

_____

_____

_____

_____

_____

_____

2 **Do not look back at the article. Are these statements about the Olympics true (T) or false (F)?**

a) Countries compete fiercely to host the Olympic games. ☐

b) Initially women were not officially allowed to compete in the modern Olympics. ☐

c) In the ancient games both men and woman could compete. ☐

d) The Olympic emblem with the five rings first appeared at the Olympic Games in 1913. ☐

e) The Olympic torch has always been part of the games. ☐

f) The games are not as popular now as they used to be. ☐

g) Choosing the host city can be difficult. ☐

h) A purpose built Olympic city is currently being planned. ☐

Read the text again and check your answers.

3 **Find words or phrases in the text which mean:**

a) intense (paragraph 1) _____

b) admiration, respect (paragraph 1) _____

c) symbol (paragraph 3) _____

d) brought back again (paragraph 4) _____

e) difficult or complicated (paragraph 6)

_____

f) to take advantage of, usually financially (paragraph 6) _____

g) who take part (paragraph 6) _____

h) as a result (paragraph 7) _____

The Changing Face of the Olympic Games

1 The history of the Olympic Games has always been closely related to the cities that have held them. This is because it's the city, and not the country, that makes the bid to host the Olympic Games. Understandably, the competition to host the Olympics is fierce, as it can bring great prestige and prosperity to the city.

2 From its rebirth in Athens in 1896 to the present day, the modern Olympic Games have gone through many changes. It was not until the Stockholm games in 1912 that women were officially admitted to the Olympics, though they had participated in some events before then. In the ancient games in Greece, women were not even allowed to watch the games, let alone take part.

3 The first Olympic emblem with its distinctive five rings was designed in 1913, although it wasn't until the Antwerp games in 1920 that it could actually be used. The five rings represent the union of the five continents of the world and the colours were chosen because at least one of the five colours exists in every flag of the world's nations.

4 The Olympic torch, which had been part of the ancient games, was reinstated as part of the opening ceremony in the 1928 games in Amsterdam. A later innovation was the idea of the torch relay (carrying a lit torch from Greece to the next Olympic venue) which was introduced in the Berlin games of 1936. The relay included some 3,000 runners who carried the torch from Greece to Germany, crossing a total of seven countries.

5 The Berlin games also saw the first live television transmission of the event and during the next 60 years of the Olympics there was an enormous growth in its popularity, with a steady increase in both the number of events and the number of countries participating. More than 200 countries competed in the Beijing Olympics in 2008.

6 The process of selecting the location for an Olympic event has become increasingly tricky due to the fierce competition among the candidate cities keen to cash in on the financial and promotional advantages of hosting the games. It has been suggested that it might be worth establishing an Olympic city, purpose built to host the games and paid for with contributions from all the participating nations. The big problem, of course, would be to decide where this city should be built.

7 So at present it looks like the games will continue to travel the world, hosted by some of the world's greatest cities and bringing in their wake both glory and disruption.

Writing

Writing a short article
Linkers
Text organisation

1 **Read the text below and choose the best discourse marker.**

Hosting the Olympics is extremely expensive.
(1) **Furthermore, / However, / On the other hand,** it can ruin the local environment. (2) **Despite / For instance, / But** greenfield sites and woodlands can be lost to urban development, which means that local residents' quality of life may be diminished. (3) **In addition, / Although / On the other hand,** it can provide a boost to the local economy, generating jobs and trade. (4) **However, / Despite / In addition,** the effects can be all too temporary, leaving a city with unwanted installations and a huge debt to pay. (5) **Nonetheless, / What's more, / For example,** with careful forward planning most of these problems can be avoided.

2 **Look at the list of changes that can occur in a city when it hosts the Olympic Games.**

a) **Decide whether you think their effect will be long-term (LT) or short-term (ST).**

b) **Decide which of the changes are benefits (+) and which are drawbacks (–).**

1 An increase in pollution and litter   _ST_ –
2 Improved sports installations _____
3 More jobs in the construction industry _____
4 Good publicity for the city _____
5 Improved roads and airports _____
6 Temporary accommodation facilities _____
7 An increase in traffic congestion _____
8 More facilities for parking cars _____
9 Massive increase in number of visitors _____
10 An increase in local trade _____
11 Security problems _____

3 **Read the following task.**

> **Your city (or a city near you) has made a bid for the Olympic Games which has been met with mixed reactions. You have been asked to write a short article for your local English language newspaper defending the bid. Your article should cover the following points:**
>
> **1** why the city would make a good venue
> **2** the construction work that would be necessary
> **3** the disruption to normal lives during the games
> **4** conclusion – the long- and short-term benefits for the city

4 **Look at the sentences below. Which point in the task could they be used to support?**

a) All in all, I think we should welcome the chance to host the games ...
b) Curiously there has been some hostility to the city's bid to host the Olympics ...
c) Although it will entail some upheaval in the short-term ...
d) However, the long-term benefits far outweigh the short-term disruption ...
e) In addition, we will need to upgrade the present infrastructure as well as ...
f) There will inevitably be some disruption to everyday lives, however ...
g) New roads will obviously be needed, as will ...
h) ... and in addition it is perfectly located ...

5 **Make brief notes on your ideas under the four headings.**

1 why the city would make a good venue

_____
_____
_____
_____
_____

2 the construction work that would be necessary

_____
_____
_____
_____
_____

3 the disruption to normal lives during the games

_____
_____
_____
_____
_____

4 conclusion – the long- and short-term benefits for the city

_____
_____
_____
_____
_____

6 **Write your article using your notes and the useful expressions from Exercises 1 and 4. You should write about 250 words.**

4 Story

Grammar

1 **Underline the correct alternative.**

a) We were on the point **of leaving** / **to leave**, when they finally arrived.

b) I was just about **to send** / **sending** the email, when I noticed I'd clicked 'reply all'.

c) The Queen was **have opened** / **to have opened** the gallery, but a security alert meant the honours were done by her secretary on her behalf.

d) I'd been thinking **to drive** / **of driving** to London, but I got the train instead.

e) Smith was on the verge **of signing** / **to sign** for Liverpool, but an eleventh-hour bid from Chelsea was too lucrative to resist.

f) Play was **resuming** / **to resume** at 1.30, but at twenty past the heavens opened yet again.

2 **Rewrite the sentences using the word in brackets so the meaning is similar.**

a) We intended to leave well before dark, but we completely lost track of time. (going)

We _____*were going to leave well before dark,*_____ but we completely lost track of time.

b) Susan had almost given up hope when the doorbell rang. (verge)

Susan _____ when the doorbell rang.

c) We wanted to set off by 5.30, but it was nearer 6.30 by the time we finally left. (hoping)

We _____ , but it was nearer 6.30 by the time we finally left.

d) I was intending not to tell him about Jack, but he insisted on hearing the whole story. (going)

I _____ , but he insisted on hearing the whole story.

e) It was originally planned that the attack would take place at nightfall, but there were last-minute concerns. (was to)

The attack _____ _____ , but there were last-minute concerns.

f) Sam was on the point of revealing everything when Miss Potts came into the room. (just about)

Sam _____ _____ when Miss Potts came into the room.

g) My parents were a little disappointed in my choice of career. I always feared this. (would)

I always feared _____ _____ in my choice of career.

h) I had planned to pay her a visit, but she had gone to her sister's for the day. (going)

I _____ , but she had gone to her sister's for the day.

3 **Complete the article with phrases using the words in the box.**

go / deliver
go / fly
verge / colonise
would / be
would / last
~~would / swallow~~
would / live

In hindsight, it's easy to scoff at past predictions

Not that many years ago, futurologists predicted that by the beginning of the 21st century we (1) _*would be swallowing*_ pills for breakfast before strapping on personal jetpacks to fly to work and that we (2) _____ in floating cities and holidaying under the sea.

Even NASA, the American space agency, was laughably wide of the mark. In 1980, it said that we (3) _____ the moon and that by the 21st century more than 1000 people would be permanently living and working there.

Other forecasts, such as the idea that by the year 2000 robots (4) _____ letters to anywhere in the world within one day, seem ridiculously naive in today's email age.

And back in the 1970s it was said that by the year 2000 computers (5) _____ as intelligent as the human brain, hypersonic aircraft (6) _____ from London to Sydney in two hours, and shoes, one pundit famously proclaimed, (7) _____ _____ a lifetime.

The only recurrent theme that emerges from years of studies looking into the future is that we are much better at creating it than we are at predicting it.

4 Complete the sentences about events or situations in your life.

a) I was once going to _____ _____ but _____ _____

b) The other day, I was just about to _____ _____ when _____

c) I always knew I'd _____ _____ _____

d) I never thought I'd _____ _____ _____

5 Match the discourse markers that have similar meanings.

a)	for example		1	in addition
b)	too		2	say
c)	strictly speaking		3	by contrast
d)	that is to say		4	particularly
e)	in particular		5	in other words
f)	including		6	likewise
g)	similarly		7	such as
h)	on the other hand		8	to be accurate

a	b	c	d	e	f	g	h
2							

6 Complete the sentences with the discourse markers in the boxes.

> likewise   ~~particularly~~   such as
> to be accurate   too

a) I love reading autobiographies, _____particularly_____ those of historical figures.

b) I really love books that keep you guessing right up to the end. _____ , stories that have a sudden and totally unexpected ending.

c) I quite like some children's books, _____ the 'Harry Potter' series. And I quite like the 'Young James Bond' books _____ .

d) All seven Harry Potter books have been made into films. _____ , there are actually eight films, as the final book is made as two separate films.

> on the other hand   or even
> strictly speaking   that is to say

e) I sometimes download films from the Internet. _____ it's illegal, but everyone does it, don't they?

f) I love all the old classic black and white films of the 40s and 50s, _____ the old silent films from the 20s if I'm in the mood.

g) The CGI (Computer Generated Imagery), _____ at least 90% of the film, has set a new standard in realism. The acting, _____ , leaves a lot to be desired.

> at any rate   in addition   say   then

h) _____ to winning the Booker prize in 1981, *Midnight's Children* by Salman Rushdie won the Best of the Bookers in 2008.

i) I've never really read any Shakespeare. Well, not from start to finish _____ .

j) You've never read *Perfume* by Patrick Suskind! You'd better come round and borrow my copy _____ . It really is an amazing book.

k) Can you recommend a good page-turner for me to take on holiday? _____ , something like *The Da Vinci Code* or that sort of thing.

7 Think of a book or a film you know. Complete the sentences about this book or film.

a) It's got *some really funny bits, such as when Jack, the main character, forgets who he is.*

b) It's got _____ , such as _____ _____

c) I like _____ _____ , particularly _____ .

d) The main character is _____ _____ He she _____ too .

e) I like _____ . On the other hand _____ _____ .

Vocabulary

1 **What kind of stories are these? Choose from the words in the boxes.**

> anecdote   fable   fairy tale   legend   myth
> news story   thriller   whodunnit   short story

a) *short story*
b) _____
c) _____
d) _____
e) _____
f) _____
g) _____
h) _____

2 **Write the names of one or two stories, books or films that you know for each of the story types.**

Fable-lit: _____
Myth: _____
Whodunnit: _____
Fairy tale: _____
Legend: _____

3 **Complete the dialogues with the expressions in the box.**

> cock and bull story   tell tales   ~~end of story~~
> it's a long story   old wives' tale   sob story
> the story of my life   to cut a long story short

a) A: Come on, you've got to tell me what happened at the party. I'm dying to know.

   B: Look, I'm not telling you. *End of story* .

b) A: So why did Jackie and Peter split up?

   B: Oh, _____ . I'll tell you about it another time.

c) A: Mummy, Evie drew on the wall at school today. But she said it was Millie who did it.

   B: Don't _____ , Lauren. I'm sure the teacher knows all about it.

d) A: Carlo reckons he was late this morning because his car wouldn't start.

   B: Huh! That's a _____ if ever I heard one. He only lives ten minutes' walk away.

e) A: You're not going to believe this! Five of my lottery numbers came up this week. But, guess what – it was the one week I didn't buy a ticket. It's _____ .

   B: Oh well, five numbers wouldn't have won that much anyway.

f) A: Mel and Jo have split up. She's really upset.

   B: Oh, she'll be OK in a day or two. She's always got some _____ about how her boyfriends keep leaving her.

g) A: How did you get that black eye?

   B: Well, _____ , Alexandra hit me.

h) A: Is it true that eating hot, spicy food makes you bad-tempered?

   B: No, it's just an _____ .

4 Complete these literary extracts with the adjectives in the box.

> astute   fishy   gullible   plausible
> sceptical   ~~unfaithful~~   unscrupulous

a) She was struck by the idea that perhaps she was being foolish in remaining faithful to her husband while Joe was so obviously _unfaithful_ to her.

b) Kate felt inordinately pleased at his offer, even though she was _____ enough to know that it came from a desire for any company, rather than hers specifically.

c) 'And you believed me?' she asked, shaking her head in disbelief.
'Give me a break! Of course I didn't. I'm not that _____ ,' came Jim's reply.

d) So he had given Katherine a call and asked if she would give him some advice on the matter. It seemed a reasonably _____ excuse for inviting her to spend more time with him.

e) 'You're completely _____ , Linda,' said Betty. 'You should be ashamed. Illegal is one thing, but immoral is another.'

f) Molly gave a _____ shrug. 'I'm really not so sure about Nicola's story. Sounds just the sort of thing she would have made up to impress Harry.'

g) There was something _____ about the whole set-up. He tried to think himself into a detective frame of mind. What would Sherlock Holmes do in the circumstances?

5 Match the words *a–g* in Exercise 4 with words *1–7* with similar meaning.

1	cynical	f		5	credible	
2	naïve			6	streetwise	
3	dubious			7	disloyal	
4	dishonest					

6 Here are some ways of responding to a story or something you hear. Match the beginnings (*a–h*) with the endings (*1–8*).

a) What a   1 no!
b) I'm not   2 you!
c) What a   3 right!
d) I don't   4 relief!
e) Lucky   5 awful!
f) Quite   6 surprised!
g) How   7 nightmare!
h) Oh   8 blame you!

a	b	c	d	e	f	g	h
4							

7 Write appropriate responses using five of the expressions from Exercise 6. More than one expression is appropriate in some cases.

a) A: Tom's house was broken into last night. I think they took quite a lot.
   B: _____ *How awful* _____ !

b) A: Sarah borrowed my camera and left it on the bus. I'm absolutely furious with her.
   B: _____ ! I would be too.

c) A: How was the flight?
   B: Don't ask! There was a last-minute delay and we spent six hours in the departure lounge.
   A: _____ !

d) A: Hey, guess who won €1000 on the lottery last night?
   B: _____ !

e) A: It's OK. They've found him safe and well.
   B: Phew! _____ !

Pronunciation

1 🔊 14 Listen to the same sentence said with the main stress in two different places. Tick the sentence in which things happened as planned and put a cross next to the sentence in which things didn't happen as planned.

a) I was <u>planning</u> to arrive at six. ☐
b) I was planning to arrive at <u>six</u>. ☐

2 🌐 15 Listen to the pairs of sentences and put a (✓) or (✗) according to whether things happened as planned, hoped etc or not.

a) i) We were planning to surprise her. ☐
   ii) We were planning to surprise her. ☐

b) i) I was hoping we'd be having pizza. ☐
   ii) I was hoping we'd be having pizza. ☐

c) i) We expected him to get grade A. ☐
   ii) We expected him to get grade A. ☐

d) i) You were supposed to dress up. ☐
   ii) You were supposed to dress up. ☐

e) i) The plane was due to arrive at 3.30. ☐
   ii) The plane was due to arrive at 3.30. ☐

f) i) I thought he'd be late. ☐
   ii) I thought he'd be late. ☐

Listen again and repeat.

Listening

1 🔵 **16 Cover the script and listen to a story called** *The Christmas Presents* **by the American author O. Henry. Answer the questions.**

a)   Who are the two main characters?

_____

b)   What is the relationship between them?

_____

c)   What are their most prized possessions?

_____

_____

d)   What Christmas presents did they buy for each other?

_____

_____

2 **Listen again. Number the events below in the order they are mentioned in the story.**

a)   Della remembered how she and Jim saw some combs in a shop window.   ☐

b)   Jim sold his watch.   ☐

c)   Della decided to sell her hair.   1

d)   Della bought a gold watch chain for Jim.   ☐

e)   Jim came home from work that evening.   ☐

f)   Della gave Jim his present.   ☐

g)   Jim opened his present.   ☐

h)   Jim gave Della her present.   ☐

i)   Della opened her present.   ☐

Did the events take place in the same order as they are described in the story?

3 **Read the story and find words or phrases that mean:**

a)   collect or gather   _____

b)   dark red   _____

c)   put on carelessly   _____

d)   walked determinedly   _____

e)   a piece of hair   _____

f)   valued greatly   _____

g)   gave   _____

h)   a quick look   _____

i)   shaking nervously   _____

j)   moved clumsily   _____

The Christmas Presents   *O Henry*

Della so wanted to get her husband Jim something special for Christmas, but the few cents she'd managed to scrape together weren't going to go very far.

As she stood in front of the mirror, her beautiful, long auburn hair hanging over her shoulders, she had an idea. She flung on her coat and marched out onto the street. She stopped in front of a door which bore a sign saying 'Hair Goods of All Kinds'. She pushed the door open and walked in.

'Will you buy my hair?' asked Della. 'Twenty dollars. Will that do you?' said the old lady. Della nodded, fighting back the tears as the first lock fell to the floor. But once she had the money in her hand, the smile returned to her face.

She knew exactly what she was looking for. The one possession that Jim prized above all others was a gold pocket watch that had been his father's and his grandfather's before him, but it had no chain. And Della wanted to buy him a simple gold chain to hold this precious watch. She handed over the twenty dollars, wrapped the chain up safely and set off for home.

On her way, she stopped to look in the window of her favourite shop. It sold antique knick-knacks and there in the window lay a set of beautiful hair combs. She and Jim had stopped here the other day to admire them. He told her that the combs would have looked beautiful against the dark red of her hair. Della caught a glimpse of her reflection in the window. What would Jim say? She was sure he'd forgive her once he saw his present. And anyway, she thought her hair looked quite good in its new, boyish style.

That evening she felt excited, and when she heard Jim's footsteps, she ran to the door. The look on his face when he saw her was a hundred times worse than anything she could have expected. His face crumpled and he reached out his hand, saying 'Your hair'.

She ran towards him, crying and apologising, 'Jim, I'm sorry, I sold it to buy you a present. Look!' and she thrust the tiny parcel in his hand. He, at the same time, reached into his pocket and held out a small parcel of about the same size.

'My darling, of course I love you, with or without your hair, it's just that I bought these for you ...'

They both took the small, simply wrapped presents from each other's trembling hands. Della opened hers. There in her hand lay the combs.

'Oh, my love,' she whispered, 'They're beautiful, but don't worry, my hair'll grow. Go on open your present ...'

His hands fumbled on the paper as he pulled out the gold chain, and his mouth shaped itself into a sad smile. 'Don't you like it?' she asked anxiously. 'It's perfect,' he said. 'But it's just that ... I sold my watch this evening ... to buy the combs!'

Writing

Writing a review

1 Read the review of another short story by O. Henry, *A Service of Love*. Which of the following information is included in the review?

a) story title and author ☐

b) brief information about the author ☐

c) when the story was written ☐

d) where and when the story is set ☐

e) overview of the story ☐

f) story synopsis/summary ☐

g) direct quotes from the story ☐

h) when the reviewer read the story ☐

i) reviewer's opinion of the story ☐

j) reviewer's recommendation ☐

2 The words a–l can be used to describe a story, book or film. Match them with the definitions 1–12. The first one has been done for you.

a) implausible ☐ 9

b) a tear-jerker ☐

c) an eye-opener ☐

d) controversial ☐

e) well-written ☐

f) far-fetched ☐

g) moving ☐

h) a slow-starter ☐

i) gripping ☐

j) thought-provoking ☐

k) unputdownable ☐

l) a page-turner ☐

1 difficult to believe because it is very unlikely

2 makes you feel emotional

3 so interesting or exciting that you do not want to stop reading it

4 another way of saying so interesting or exciting that you do not want to stop reading it

5 written in a way that is skilful, effective or successful

6 very exciting and interesting and keeps your attention

7 not very interesting or exciting at the beginning, but becoming more so later

8 reveals surprising things that you did not know before

9 difficult to accept as true

10 about a subject or gives an opinion that people disagree with or do not approve of

11 sad and maybe makes you cry

12 makes you think of new ideas or changes your attitude to something

3 You are going to write a review of either *The Christmas Presents* on page 26 or a story of your choice (a short story, book or film).

- Include the relevant information in Exercise 1.
- Make notes on the information you are going to include.
- Try to include some of the words a–l in Exercise 2 when giving your opinion of the story.
- Write the review in no more than 250 words.

REVIEW: *A Service of Love*

A Service of Love is a short story written by the famous American short-story writer O. Henry.

THE STORY is about a couple who lie to each other about their jobs until events force them to admit the truth. It is set in the USA in the late 1800s.

The story begins with two would-be artists, Joe and Delia, who do not know each other and who both move from the country to New York. They meet, fall in love and get married. They soon realize that their small-town talents are not enough to bring them success in the big city, so they both get other jobs. However, they still believe in their partner's abilities, and in order not to disappoint each other, they lie about their jobs; Joe keeps up the pretence that he's making money from painting and Delia pretends to be giving piano lessons. In reality they are both working in the same laundry, Joe in the boiler room and Delia upstairs ironing clothes.

One day Delia burns her hand and uses a rag from the boiler room as a bandage. She lies to Joe about her injury, but he recognises the rag. The couple then confess their secret lives to each other, realising that their love is far more important than their art.

This is a great little story and is typical of O. Henry in being slightly implausible but very enjoyable, with its clever and unexpected twist at the end. Despite being a short story, the imagery is very vivid and you feel empathy for the main characters from the very beginning.

I would certainly recommend this story to anyone, without telling them the ending of course.

5 Bargain

Grammar

1 Underline the correct alternative in these news stories.

FLOWER POWER

A florist's in Coventry is offering bunches of dead roses wrapped in black paper for jilted lovers to send to their ex-partners. The owner says the inspiration for the idea was her partner, **she split up with last month / whom she split up with last month**.

SECURITY RISK

A shoplifter was yesterday given a six-week jail sentence by a court in Rotherham after he removed a security tag from an item of clothing and tried to walk out of the shop with it so it couldn't be used as evidence. "It's not something **I'm proud of / of I'm proud**," Paul Wood, 26, said as he left the court. It is the fifth shoplifting offence **of which Wood has been convicted / which Wood has been convicted**.

COUNTING ON THE MONEY

A woman from Dewsbury, **whom Dracula and vampires have been a life-long obsession for / for whom Dracula and vampires have been a life-long obsession**, has set up a company which imports and sells coffins from Transylvania. The company sells five different products, **the most popular of which is painted blood red / of the most popular which is painted blood red**.

HITTING THE JACKPOT

A man **whom the local golf club was a second home for / for whom the local golf club was a second home**, and who took his wife to bingo only to stop her complaining, has won the £200,000 jackpot at a club in Bristol. And what is the lucky Mr Jones going to treat himself to first? "There's a new set of clubs **for I've been saving up / I've been saving up for**," he said.

2 Rewrite the sentences to make them more formal or informal.

a) This is the shop from which I got my camera.
This is the shop I got my camera from.

b) Is this the hotel in which we stayed last year?
_____

c) Jo is someone you can always rely on.
_____

d) It's technically a crime, but nothing you'd be arrested for.
_____

e) The person to whom you need to speak is not here at the moment.
_____
_____

f) Are they the people Luke went on holiday with?
_____
_____

3 Which of the twelve sentences in Exercise 2 are formal (*F*) and which are informal (*I*)?

4 Rewrite the sentences as one sentence using a non-defining relative clause.

a) He earns about $200 a week. He spends most of it on computer games.
He earns about $200 a week, most of which he spends on computer games.

b) I've got a few friends in the UK. Most of them live in London.
_____
_____

c) We made loads of food for the party. Most of it didn't get eaten.
_____
_____

d) There are about forty university colleges in Oxford. The oldest is Balliol College.
_____
_____

e) We've got exams all next week. The first exam is maths.
_____
_____

5 Complete the texts by adding *a/an, the* or leaving the space blank.

Famous business decisions – good and bad

a In 2003, _–_ Manchester United bought Portuguese footballer Cristiano Ronaldo as _____ replacement for David Beckham. _____ club paid £12 million for Ronaldo. In _____ June 2009, Ronaldo was sold to _____ Real Madrid for £80 million, giving the club _____ profit of £68 million on _____ top of _____ three league titles and six trophies they won while he was playing for them.

b Swiss watches and _____ companies making them used to be _____ envy of _____ world. However, primarily due to strong competition from _____ Japanese companies during _____ 1970s and 80s, sales of _____ Swiss watches worldwide fell drastically. _____ Swiss and _____ Japanese decided to collaborate and the result was _____ product called 'Swatch'. Today 'Swatch' accounts for _____ 50% of all _____ watches sold.

c In _____ early 1950s, smalltime record producer Sam Phillips had _____ exclusive contract with _____ young unknown singer he had discovered. In 1955, he sold _____ contract to _____ RCA record company for _____ $35,000. That singer was Elvis Presley and Phillips lost _____ income from over _____ billion records, CDs and downloads.

d In 1888, businessman Asa Chandler bought _____ rights to _____ Coca-Cola from its inventor, John Pemberton. This is generally regarded as one of _____ best business decisions ever made. However, ten years later, in one of _____ worst business decisions ever, Chandler sold _____ bottling rights for just $1. Today, _____ billion units of Coca-Cola are produced each day.

e In one of _____ most infamous business decisions ever made, Decca Records turned down _____ Beatles in _____ January 1962. After _____ 15-song audition at Decca studios, _____ company told _____ group's manager, Brian Epstein, 'We don't like your boys' sound. _____ groups are out; four-piece groups with _____ guitars particularly are finished.'

🔊 **17 Listen and check.**

6 Underline the <u>two</u> correct alternatives in the sentences.

a) I'm going to the **work** / <u>**office**</u> / **bed** / <u>**shops**</u>.

b) William's not here. He's at **shop** / **gym** / **home** / **school**.

c) I'm going to **theatre** / **work** / **school** / **gym** later.

d) Let's meet outside **library** / **Tom's house** / **Café Coco** / **café** at 7.30.

e) Alex has gone to the **café** / **bed** / **home** / **cinema**.

f) I'd like to work for the **police** / **education** / **law** / **government**.

g) I don't like the **Brahms's music** / **music of Brahms** / **Brahms 4th symphony** / **Brahms you were playing last night**.

h) When did you leave **party** / **university** / **school** / **shops**?

i) I've always loved the **paella** / **paella for lunch** / **paella in this restaurant** / **paella my mother makes**.

7 Complete the gap with *a/an* or *the*, or leave it blank.

a) I live in _the_ south of the UK. In a small village _____ south of Winchester.

b) We usually have _____ lunch at home, but we're going out for _____ surprise birthday lunch for my mum today.

c) I hardly ever go anywhere by _____ bus. In fact, I last went on _____ bus about a year ago.

d) We've put off the party till _____ next weekend because that's _____ weekend my brother and his family are visiting us.

e) I buy things on _____ Internet all the time. _____ Internet shopping is fantastic.

f) I hope that one day we may have _____ world without crime or violence or wars. One day we may have _____ world peace.

g) People say _____ French often criticise foreigners who speak _____ French, but I have never found that to be true.

Pronunciation

Look at the sentences below. Decide whether *the* is pronounced as /ðə/ or /ði/.

a) The TV remote control is on the table.

b) Is the umbrella in the hall?

c) This is the oldest building in the city.

d) Don't use the printer. The ink's running out.

e) The ice-rink is next to the park. Just before the university.

f) The exam's on the 8th. In the afternoon.

g) The film was great. The scene at the end was amazing.

🔊 **18 Listen and check. Repeat the sentences.**

Vocabulary

1 Combine words in box A with those in box B to make expressions connected with money. Then use these expressions to complete the sentences.

A

| shop | ~~make~~ | impulse | slap-up | down- |

B

| around | meal | ~~do~~ | buy | payment |

a) I can't afford a new pair of jeans. I'll have to __make do__ with these old ones for while longer.

b) It's always a good idea to _____ and compare prices before you buy anything.

c) I've never ever worn this pink and orange shirt. It was an _____ last summer. I thought it looked cool at the time.

d) Hey, let's celebrate the end of the exams with a _____ at that new restaurant.

e) If you can't afford to pay in full, you can always make a _____ of say 10% to reserve the item.

2 Write true answers to the questions.

a) Have you ever paid over the odds for something? What was it?

_____

b) When did you last have a slap-up meal?

_____

c) Do you generally live within your means?

_____

d) Name something that in your opinion is generally overpriced.

_____

e) Name something that in your opinion is exorbitantly priced.

_____

f) Have you ever made an impulse buy? What was it?

_____

3 Look at this extract from a radio programme and complete what Steve says with the correct form of the phrasal verbs in the box.

come in	cut back	get around	get by
~~get into~~	live on	pay off	run up
save up	splash out		

Presenter: As part of our feature on student life, we're talking about money. With me first off today is Steve, who's just left university. So, Steve, how is it being a student these days, financially speaking?

Steve: Well, in a word, it's not great. I mean you (1) __get into__ debt before you've even started. You get a student loan but it really isn't enough to (2) _____ , so you have to get overdrafts and perhaps further loans. So most students have (3) _____ even more debts by the time they leave.

Presenter: And was that the case for you?

Steve: Well, I started off spending without thinking, you know, (4) _____ on this and that. But I soon realised that I was going to have to (5) _____ on much, much less each week. Also, I originally thought I'd be able to (6) _____ to go away in the summer holidays, but that was never going to happen.

Presenter: So, what did you do to start economising?

Steve: I started (7) _____ on what I spent by, say, buying supermarket own brands, buying stuff in bulk, not going out so often and that sort of thing. And I brought my old bike from home so I could (8) _____ without using the bus.

Presenter: And how did you manage?

Steve: Well, I just about coped, although I have to say that my parents (9) _____ useful from time to time with the odd bit of financial help. All in all, my university days were brilliant, but it was hard having no money. I'm working now, but I'm still (10) _____ my student loan though.

🌀 **19 Listen and check.**

4 Complete the expressions using the words in the box.

the red	cost	frills	off	robbery

a) My account is always in _____ . I think I've got an overdraft limit of £1000 and I often get close to that.

b) All these low _____ , no-_____ airlines are pretty cheap, but the service is pretty dreadful too from my experience.

c) Fifty euros for that! What a rip-_____ ! It's not worth twenty. It's daylight _____ .

5 Complete the dialogues by choosing the best alternative.

a) A: I'm always _____*broke*_____ these days.
   B: Get a new job. Or start spending less.
   broke / thrifty / frugal

b) A: There are some great bargains in that clothes shop on Market Street. Most things are _____ by at least 50%.
   B: Great. I'll try and get there later.
   short of money / affordable / discounted

c) A: How was Suzy and Harry's wedding?
   B: Amazing – incredibly _____ . I dread to think how much it cost.
   exorbitant / lavish / generous

d) A: What's that new restaurant like?
   B: Not bad. And pretty _____ too.
   discounted / budget / affordable

e) A: Shall we try that new restaurant tonight?
   B: I hear it's a bit _____ . Maybe we should save it for a special occasion.
   overpriced / affordable / no-frills

f) A: It cost €300 to fix my computer.
   B: How much? That's _____ . It should've been a hundred at the absolute most.
   lavish / upmarket / exorbitant

g) A: How do you manage to travel abroad for so long on so little money?
   B: You have to be _____ – cheap hotels, get the bus not the train and eat cheaply.
   frugal / affordable / lavish

6 Rearrange the words in brackets to complete the conversation between a customer and a market stall holder.

Woman: Excuse me, how much is this necklace?

Man: That's £200.

Woman: Oh, (1) _____ _____ (I / than / pay / a bit / to / that's / more / was / prepared)

Man: It's solid silver, madam. £200 is a good price.

Woman: (2) _____ _____ ? (give / me / Could / discount / a / you)

Man: Well alright, for you, £175.

Woman: I'm afraid (3) _____ _____ (a bit / range / it's / price / above / still / my)

Man: OK, I'll do you a special price of £150.

Woman: (4) _____ ? (that / price / your / best / Is)

Man: Yes, it is madam.

Woman: (5) _____ , thanks. (then / leave / it / I / I'll / think)

Man: OK, (6) _____ _____ ? (want / pay / how / you / to / do / much)

Woman: I'm prepared to give you £100.

Man: Make it £120 and we've got a deal.

Woman: (7) _____ . Thank you. (I'll / it / Right / take)

🔊 **20 Listen and check.**

Reading

1 🔊 21 Read the news story at the bottom of the page. What connects the items in the pictures?

2 Answer the questions in your own words.

   a) What were Kyle MacDonald's living arrangements a year ago?

   b) Why was it difficult for him to buy his own home?

   c) What was MacDonald's idea?

   d) How did a children's game help him?

   e) Why did people think MacDonald had gone mad?

   f) Who is going to have the film role?

   g) What surprised MacDonald?

   h) What is MacDonald planning to do with the original red paper clip?

3 The word *trade* is used as both a noun and verb several times in the article. Underline two other words in the article with a similar meaning to *trade*.

4 Find words or phrases in the article to match the definitions *a–j*.

   a) start something in order to achieve an aim (para 1) _____

   b) something that you hope to achieve (para 1) _____

   c) not possible (para 2) _____

   d) start or create something (para 3) _____

   e) started behaving in a strange or silly way (para 4) _____

   f) a group of similar or connected things (para 5) _____

   g) new or unusual (para 5) _____

   h) slightly strange (para 5) _____

   i) made people feel enthusiastic about something (para 5) _____

   j) a party that you give in a house that you have just moved into (para 6) _____

Man turns paper clip into house

A man who set out to use the internet to trade a red paper clip for a house has achieved his goal and is now a home-owner.

Kyle MacDonald, 26, from British Columbia, Canada, was living in rented accommodation with his girlfriend and decided it was time they owned their own home. But on MacDonald's pay as a pizza delivery man buying one was out of the question.

MacDonald got the idea from the children's game 'Bigger and Better'. He set up the website oneredpaperclip.com, which offered to trade a red paper clip for something 'more valuable'. MacDonald would then trade that item and so on until he had traded up to a house. From paper clip to house took fifteen trades and exactly one year.

The first swap was for a fish-shaped pen, which in turn was traded for a hand-made ceramic doorknob. Subsequent trades included a camping stove, a snowmobile, a trip to Russia, a recording contract and an afternoon with rock star Alice Cooper. However, MacDonald's followers thought he'd lost the plot when he opted to trade the latter for a snow globe. But his fans need not have worried. Hollywood director Corbin Bernsen collects snow globes and wanted it so much that he exchanged it for a paid, credited, speaking role in his next film. The house, in Kipling, Saskatchewan, was offered by the town's Mayor in exchange for the film role, for which any of Kipling's inhabitants will be able to audition.

MacDonald's achievement is the latest in a string of novel and quirky ideas that demonstrate the power of the internet. 'I knew it was possible. You can do anything if you put your mind to it,' says MacDonald. But he remains surprised at the level of publicity generated. 'A lot of people have been asking how I've stirred up so much publicity around the project, and my simple answer is: 'I have no idea.''

MacDonald and his girlfriend are currently organising a housewarming party and are hoping that all the traders will attend. The couple are then planning to get married. 'The wedding ring is going to be made out of the original red paper clip,' MacDonald said.

Writing

Writing a news story
Features of a news story
Paragraph organisation

1 **Look at the news story 'Man turns paper clip into house' on page 32 and put the following paragraph summaries into the order in which they occur.**

   a) Kyle MacDonald's plans for the future ☐

   b) Details about the trades ☐

   c) Kyle MacDonald's feelings about the trades ☐

   d) Brief summary of the story ☐

   e) Background information about Kyle MacDonald ☐

   f) The idea and how it came about ☐

2 **You are going to write a news story called 'Man sells life on eBay'. Follow the instructions below.**

   a) Read the notes and make sure you have a clear picture of the story.

   b) Decide which of the following is the most suitable paragraph for summarising the story.

      (i) A Briton living in Australia has recently split up with his wife of five years and decided to sell all his possessions that reminded him of her.

      (ii) Ian Usher, 44, a Briton living in Australia has sold his 'entire life' on eBay for AU$ 399,000 because he has recently split up with his wife of five years.

      (iii) A Briton living in Australia has agreed a bid of more than AU$ 399,000 after putting his 'entire life' up for sale following a recent split from his wife.

   c) Decide on a suitable order for the following paragraphs.

      Ian Usher's feelings about the sale ☐

      The idea and why it came about ☐

      A brief summary of the story ☐

      The events of the actual sale ☐

      Ian Usher's plans for the future ☐

      Details about what was for sale ☐

      Background information about Ian Usher ☐

   d) Plan the content of the paragraphs for your news story. Think about how to expand the notes into complete sentences and how to connect the sentences. You can use one of the summary paragraphs above if you like.

   e) Write your news story. You should write about 250 words.

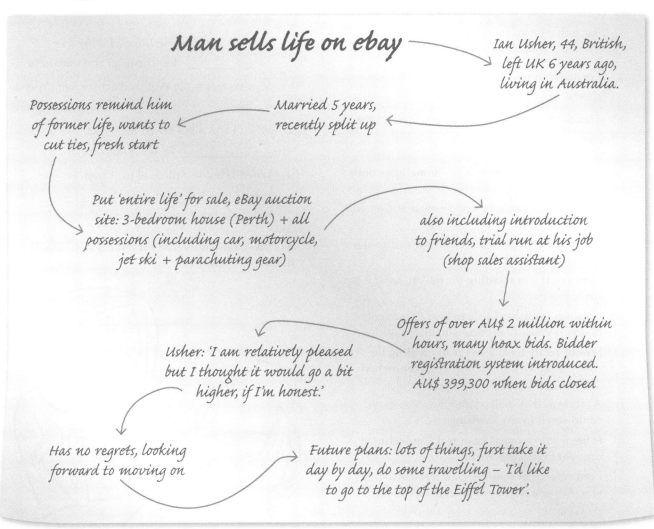

Man sells life on ebay

Ian Usher, 44, British, left UK 6 years ago, living in Australia.

Married 5 years, recently split up

Possessions remind him of former life, wants to cut ties, fresh start

Put 'entire life' for sale, eBay auction site: 3-bedroom house (Perth) + all possessions (including car, motorcycle, jet ski + parachuting gear)

also including introduction to friends, trial run at his job (shop sales assistant)

Offers of over AU$ 2 million within hours, many hoax bids. Bidder registration system introduced. AU$ 399,300 when bids closed

Usher: 'I am relatively pleased but I thought it would go a bit higher, if I'm honest.'

Has no regrets, looking forward to moving on

Future plans: lots of things, first take it day by day, do some travelling – 'I'd like to go to the top of the Eiffel Tower'.

6 Mind

Grammar

1 Some of these sentences have mistakes in them. Tick the correct sentences and correct the ones that are wrong.

a) What do you fancy doing? ~~I'm feeling~~ like going to the cinema. ___*I feel*___

b) I'm feeling a bit unwell today. I think it must be the change in the weather. _____

c) If you'd been hearing the instructions, you'd know what to do. _____

d) He was hearing strange noises coming from the cellar, so he grabbed a torch and climbed down to investigate. _____

e) I've been hearing quite a lot from Dave recently. He e-mails me every day. _____

f) I think I'm smelling something burning. Are you sure you switched the cooker off?

_____

g) I'm just tasting the sauce. I think it needs more cheese. _____

h) This fish is tasting funny. Are you sure it's OK to eat? _____

2 Underline the correct verb form. Sometimes both are possible.

a) I'm hearing / <u>can hear</u> a noise outside. Can you see if it's the cat?

b) She **couldn't taste / didn't taste** the salt so she decided to add a bit more.

c) I **can smell / 'm smelling** the milk to see if it is fresh.

d) He wasn't **hearing / able to hear** the song that clearly because of the noise in the background.

e) I **could really feel / I was really feeling** the cold yesterday. I'm sure the temperature had dropped below zero.

f) As soon as they walked into the room they **could smell / were smelling** gas.

g) Is the window open? I **can feel / 'm feeling** a draught from somewhere.

h) I **can sense / 'm sensing** some resistance from you. Are you not happy with the idea?

3 Complete the sentences with an appropriate verb of the senses. You may also need to use *can, could* or *be able to*.

a) I love ___*listening*___ to music when I'm working. It really helps me concentrate.

b) I _____ the noise of the traffic from my bed, but it doesn't stop me from sleeping.

c) I can never tell the difference between cheap wines and expensive wines. They all _____ the same to me.

d) You _____ the tension in the air whenever the boss is around.

e) I _____ particularly energetic today. I don't know why!

f) I _____ perfectly until the age of 30, then my eyesight started to deteriorate quite quickly.

g) I don't like strong perfumes, I think they _____ too chemical and unnatural.

h) My eyes get really tired and achy when I spend too long _____ at a computer screen.

i) When I was a kid I used to sit and _____ TV for hours on end.

j) When I choose a piece of fruit from the fruit bowl, I love to hold it and _____ its weight in my hand before I eat it.

Are these sentences true for you? If not, rewrite them so that they are.

4 Read the text below and underline the most appropriate participle clause.

Pushy passengers win airline dispute

Fifty-four budget airline passengers, (1) **spending / <u>having spent</u> / spent** three hours waiting at Heathrow Airport, were finally informed that their flight had been cancelled due to technical problems. On (2) **hearing / having heard / heard** the news, one of the older passengers marched up to the airline office, (3) **demanding / having demanded / demanded** that they all be put on the next possible flight. However, (4) **overbooking / having overbooked / overbooked** the next flight, there was very little the airline could do.

The passengers all crowded around the airline desk, (5) **shouting and protesting / having shouted and protested / shouted and protested**. They threatened to block access to the other passengers trying to reach the check-in desks. Finally, (6) **wanted / having wanted / wanting** to do something to appease the angry crowd, the airline offered all the passengers free flights to the destination of their choice. (7) **Appeasing / Having appeased / Appeased** by this offer, they calmed down, took their seats and waited another three hours before they eventually took off, more than six hours late.

🌐 **22 Listen and check.**

5 Rewrite the sentences using a participle clause.

a) He hadn't really understood what she'd said, so he did the exercise incorrectly.
   Not having understood what she'd said, he did
   the exercise incorrectly.

b) He's English, so he finds it hard to follow them when they start speaking Czech.
   Being English, he finds it hard to follow them
   when they start speaking Czech.

c) We worked really hard at the meeting, so we all went out for a meal on the company.

d) He doesn't know the area very well, so there's a danger he'll get lost.

e) He was cleared of theft by the courts and immediately got his old job back.

f) He was lost in thought and didn't notice that his train had pulled out of the station.

g) She wasn't particularly interested in the talk and decided not to go.

h) James was delayed by the traffic on the motorway, so he was extremely late.

i) She was intrigued by the news and wanted to know more.

j) She didn't make a very good impression at the interview and was worried that she wouldn't get the job.

Vocabulary

1 Look at the anagrams. Rearrange the letters to make verbs associated with seeing. Use the clues to help you.

a) zega   look thoughtfully for a long time

    gaze

b) menixae   look closely or analytically

    _____

c) conrigese   understand what or who you can see

    _____

d) ratd   your eyes do this when they move around quickly

    _____

e) rbeosve   watch or notice

    _____

f) cnas   look over something quickly

    _____

2 Underline the correct alternative.

a) The doctor **gazed / <u>examined</u> / observed** the X-ray very carefully before speaking.

b) He panicked, his eyes **darting / gazing / scanning** from side to side, looking for a way out.

c) He looked at me for a long time and then shook his head. He really didn't seem to **scan / examine / recognise** me.

d) She stood back and **gazed / observed / scanned** the scene in the room, happy not to be part of it for the moment.

e) He **scanned / observed / recognised** the newspaper, looking for the article they'd just mentioned.

f) She **examined / gazed / darted** out of the window at the pouring rain, thinking of anything but the lesson going on around her.

3 Replace a word in these sentences with *observe, see* or *recognise.*

a) I admit that it's not an easy language to learn.
    _recognise_____

b) He doesn't really understand what you are trying to say.
    _____

c) Writing in *The Times*, Steadman wrote that Smart's latest novel was a great disappointment.
    _____

d) They have finally acknowledged his effort in the peacekeeping process.
    _____

e) 'You don't seem to be taking your studies very seriously,' remarked the teacher.
    _____

f) She said she was thinking of meeting Massimo later that evening.
    _____

g) In our family we like to follow all the old New Year traditions.
    _____

h) The government have realised that they need to put more funding into education.
    _____

4 Complete the sentences with the words in the box.

addiction	docile	nap	overcome
~~phobia~~	spotted	tattered	

a) I've got a ___*phobia*___ about cockroaches. I can't stand the sight of them.

b) She was totally _____ by emotion and couldn't hold back her tears.

c) You look tired. Why don't you have a _____ for twenty minutes?

d) Sam's dog is very _____ . He sleeps all day and lets the children climb all over him.

e) With Michaela's _____ to chocolate, it's no wonder she's putting on weight.

f) What have you done to that book? Look at the state of it. It's all _____ .

g) Can you wait a minute? I think I just _____ Rick in the next room. I need to speak to him.

5 Complete these expressions with *mind* using the words in the box.

| alike | ~~how~~ | off | on | out |
| over | own | two | | |

a) mind _how_ you go

b) mind your _____ business

c) I'm in _____ minds

d) take your mind _____ something

e) go _____ of your mind

f) Great minds think _____ .

g) mind _____ matter

h) the last thing _____ my mind

6 Complete the sentences with the expressions in Exercise 5. Make any changes that are necessary.

a) Holidays? You want to book some holidays? I'm sorry, that really is *the last thing on my mind* at the moment.

b) I don't mean to sound rude, but you know, she really does ask too many personal questions. I wish she'd learn to _____

_____ .

c) I'm _____ about this job offer. I really don't know what to do. They want an answer today but I need more time to think .

d) Come on, we can do it. Let's give it one more try. Jon, you take that side, I'll take this one. And remember, it's a question of _____

_____ !

e) _____ . It's been snowing all night and the roads will be icy.

f) Hey! Is that your new phone? I've got exactly the same one. Well, you know what they say, _____ .

g) Where have you been? Do you know what time it is? I was _____

with worry!

h) Come on! Let's go away for a couple of days. It'll help you _____ things.

7 Rearrange the words to form questions.

a) tomorrow leave Is I until it this if OK ?
Is it OK if I leave this until tomorrow?

b) please that, repeating mind you Would ?

_____

c) husband May me bring I my with ?

_____

d) I mind smoke table at if the you Do ?

_____

e) awfully mind volume turning Would a little you the down ?

_____

_____

f) please swap with seats, Can you I ?

_____

8 Match the requests (*a–f*) in Exercise 7 to these responses (1–6).

1 I'm sorry, but I need to sit at the end of the row.

2 I'd really prefer it if you could do it today.

3 Why don't you just move a bit further away? This *is* a public place, you know.

4 Why? I think I made my message very clear.

5 Not if you open the window a little.

6 Of course, he's very welcome.

a	b	c	d	e	f
2					

🔊 23 Listen and check.

Pronunciation

1 Write the noun form of the verbs and adjectives below. Sometimes there are two possible forms.

a) stimulate _____ *stimulation* _____

b) observe _____

c) recognise _____

d) active _____

e) regular _____

f) creative _____

g) popular _____

h) perfect _____

i) familiar _____

j) anxious _____

2 Mark the stress on all the words in Exercise 1.

🔊 24 Listen and check. Notice how the stress changes in the nouns.

Listening

1   🌐 25 **Cover the script opposite and listen to three people talking about stress. Make notes on the following questions.**

   a)   What is the cause of their stress?

     Mark: _____

     Kay: _____

     Liz: _____

   b)   How does it affect them?

     Mark: _____

     Kay: _____

     Liz: _____

   c)   Make a note of two things they each do to counter the stress.

     Mark: _____

     Kay: _____

     Liz: _____

2   **Listen again. Which of the three people, Mark (M), Kay (K) or Liz (L):**

   a)   suffers from the emotional effects of stress? ☐

   b)   finds that noise can be a source of stress? ☐

   c)   suffer from the physical effects of stress? ☐ ☐

   d)   doesn't like spending free time talking about work? ☐

   e)   combats stress with physical activities? ☐

   f)   feels the need to do something intellectually challenging? ☐

   g)   combats stress with social activities? ☐

   h)   combats stress with domestic activities? ☐

3   **Find words or phrases in the recording script that mean:**

   a)   to relax (Mark) _____

   b)   unable to sit still because they're nervous or bored (Mark) _____

   c)   escape (Mark) _____

   d)   held back, shut in (Mark) _____

   e)   so boring it makes you depressed (Kay) _____

   f)   without energy (Kay) _____

   g)   to lie or sit with knees pulled up so as to make yourself comfortable (Kay) _____

   h)   becoming soft and liquid (Liz) _____

Mark   Well, I suppose my job is pretty stressful. All medical staff have pretty stressful jobs, but working in the Accident and Emergency department is particularly bad. We have to be ready to react quickly and efficiently, and often people's lives are at stake. Sometimes it can  be really exhilarating, but it's also exhausting, both mentally and physically. I find it really difficult to unwind when I go home, I mean, I can't just go home and sit down and watch TV, or, or read a book, I'm too tense and get really fidgety. Some people find it's good to talk about their work – you know, go out for a couple of drinks after work and all that, but I don't. I prefer to get away from it, do some sport, maybe go running, go to the gym or play a game of squash. Squash is really good. You can thrash out all the pent-up stress and release all that tension and I find it really helps me just empty my mind and switch off.

Kay   I live about sixty miles away from where I work, and I commute in and out every day on a really busy commuter train. Sometimes there's nowhere to sit down and you have to stand up all the way. I find it really stressful. There are mobile  phones ringing all the time, and kids listening to their mp3 players, and the sight of all those bored, grey faces is really soul-destroying. After a long day at work I get home feeling totally drained and it often gives me a headache. I usually run a hot bath, play some soft music and curl up with a good book for an hour or so, and that really helps. That and cooking – I find that all the preparation involved really helps me unwind.

Liz   I've got two little boys. One's just turned two and the other's nine months old. They're lovely kids, but sometimes they just totally exhaust me! They continually want attention, whether they're hungry or tired or just bored. And I know I'm really lucky 'cos I can afford  not to go to work, so I get to spend all day with them, and that a lot of mothers have to share their energy between work and being with the children, but sometimes I really miss adult company ... being around kids all day can make you feel pretty stupid ... I sometimes feel like my brain is turning to pulp. Sometimes, when I'm really tired and stressed out I just sit down and cry. When it gets that bad, I leave the kids with their grandmother and dedicate a day to my mind! Going to a film, or an art exhibition, reading the newspaper from cover to cover or maybe just meeting a friend for a long lunch and some adult conversation.

Writing

Writing an informal email offering advice
Paragraph organisation
Useful phrases for offering advice

1 Steve receives an email from his friend, Fran. Read the email. What do you think Fran must have said to him in her email?

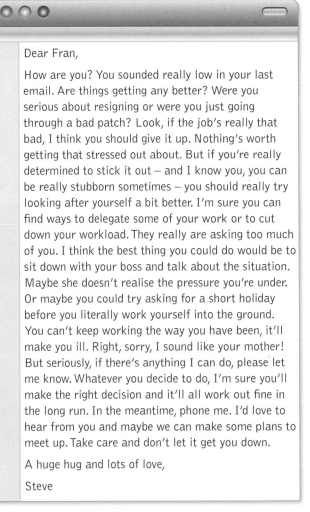

Dear Fran,

How are you? You sounded really low in your last email. Are things getting any better? Were you serious about resigning or were you just going through a bad patch? Look, if the job's really that bad, I think you should give it up. Nothing's worth getting that stressed out about. But if you're really determined to stick it out – and I know you, you can be really stubborn sometimes – you should really try looking after yourself a bit better. I'm sure you can find ways to delegate some of your work or to cut down your workload. They really are asking too much of you. I think the best thing you could do would be to sit down with your boss and talk about the situation. Maybe she doesn't realise the pressure you're under. Or maybe you could try asking for a short holiday before you literally work yourself into the ground. You can't keep working the way you have been, it'll make you ill. Right, sorry, I sound like your mother! But seriously, if there's anything I can do, please let me know. Whatever you decide to do, I'm sure you'll make the right decision and it'll all work out fine in the long run. In the meantime, phone me. I'd love to hear from you and maybe we can make some plans to meet up. Take care and don't let it get you down.

A huge hug and lots of love,

Steve

2 Look at Steve's email again. Divide the letter into three paragraphs.

Paragraph 1: Steve (1) responds directly to what Fran said in her email and (2) offers sympathy and understanding.

Paragraph 2: Steve (1) offers some concrete advice as to how to improve the situation and (2) warns her about the consequences for her health.

Paragraph 3: Steve (1) makes a funny remark to lighten the tone, (2) lets her know he believes in her ability to cope with the situation and (3) offers to help if he can.

3 Look at the email again and underline all the expressions Steve uses to give advice. Can you think of any more useful phrases for giving advice?

4 A friend of yours, Jane, wrote you the following email. She's obviously under a lot of stress. Read the email and answer the following questions.

a) What is the cause of her stress?

b) What effect is it having on her?

c) What advice did her boyfriend give her? Do you agree with his advice?

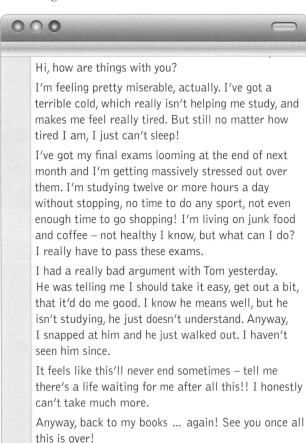

Hi, how are things with you?

I'm feeling pretty miserable, actually. I've got a terrible cold, which really isn't helping me study, and makes me feel really tired. But still no matter how tired I am, I just can't sleep!

I've got my final exams looming at the end of next month and I'm getting massively stressed out over them. I'm studying twelve or more hours a day without stopping, no time to do any sport, not even enough time to go shopping! I'm living on junk food and coffee – not healthy I know, but what can I do? I really have to pass these exams.

I had a really bad argument with Tom yesterday. He was telling me I should take it easy, get out a bit, that it'd do me good. I know he means well, but he isn't studying, he just doesn't understand. Anyway, I snapped at him and he just walked out. I haven't seen him since.

It feels like this'll never end sometimes – tell me there's a life waiting for me after all this!! I honestly can't take much more.

Anyway, back to my books ... again! See you once all this is over!

Jane

5 Which of the following points would you include in a reply to Jane's email? Is there anything else you would like to add?

a) She must try to eat properly, it'll give her more energy.

b) Doing sport really helps boost energy levels and clear the mind.

c) Seeing people is really important to stop her from getting depressed and touchy.

d) Studying in short bursts and taking short breaks is far more efficient than slogging away for hours on end.

e) She's a good student and has never failed an exam in her life, why should she fail now?

f) You were in the same position last year so you understand exactly how she feels.

g) Offer to cook for her for a week.

6 Write an email to Jane. Be comforting without sounding too pushy. Use Steve's letter and the useful phrases in Exercise 3 to help you. You should write between 200 and 250 words.

7 Digital

Grammar

1 Combine the short sentences to make one complex sentence. Use the framework given below and write no more than three words in each gap.

> • Netbooks are inexpensive and light.
> • Netbooks appeal to a wide audience.
> • They appeal to business people who travel frequently.
> • They appeal to kids and home users.
> • They are looking for a small laptop.
> • They want to be able to carry it from room to room.
> • They also appeal to students.
> • They have to carry heavy books around with them all day.
> • They don't want the extra weight of a full size laptop.

Inexpensive and (1) _____ ,
netbooks appeal to a very wide audience, from
(2) _____ travel
frequently to kids (3) _____
users looking (4) _____
laptop which they (5) _____
from room to room, to students who
(6) _____ heavy books
around all day and (7) _____
the extra weight of a full size laptop.

> • Speech recognition has reached an important point in its development.
> • With speech recognition you can navigate your computer without a key board and mouse.
> • You can also write documents without using the keyboard and mouse.
> • It's much faster with speech recognition.

(8) _____ has
reached the point where you can actually
(9) _____ and
(10) _____ faster than
(11) _____ with a (12) _____
_____ .

2 Look again at the short sentences in the boxes in Exercise 1. Cross out all the words and expressions that are not used in the longer sentences.

3 Write the phrases in the correct order to complete the complex sentences.

a) The perfect computer would be one …
/ and light / that is so small / can open out /
it can fit comfortably in your pocket, /
to give you / but at the same time /
a full size screen / .

that is so small _____
_____
_____
_____

b) I think speech recognition could …
/ with physical disabilities / do so many good
things, / to access / quickly and easily /
all the functions on their computer /
such as help people / .

_____
_____
_____
_____

c) I would love to have …
/ that can park itself, / in the parking space/
lining itself up / and doing / for me! /
all that awkward manoeuvring / a car /

_____
_____
_____
_____

4 Write complex sentences that are true for you. Use the sentence openings below and try to include as much information as possible.

a) The next electronic device I buy will be a _____
_____
_____
_____

b) My idea of the perfect holiday is _____
_____
_____
_____

5 Look at these pairs of sentences. Is the meaning similar (S) or different (D)?

1 a) We'll probably have to eat less meat and fish as the agricultural industry cuts back on its carbon footprint.

   b) It is likely we'll be eating less meat and fish as the agricultural industry cuts back on its carbon footprint. [S]

2 a) We're bound to see someone we know at the party.

   b) We may well see someone we know at the party. [ ]

3 a) He could easily change his mind tomorrow when he sees how challenging the course is.

   b) He definitely won't be of the same opinion tomorrow when he sees how challenging the course is. [ ]

4 a) Experts believe that it is highly likely that the present generation of children will have an average life expectancy of over 100 years.

   b) Experts believe that the present generation of children may possibly live to be over 100. [ ]

5 a) It is highly unlikely that a cure will ever be found for the common cold.

   b) We'll probably never find a cure for the common cold. [ ]

Where the two sentences have a different meaning, rewrite sentence (b) so that it has a similar meaning to sentence (a), but using a different future expression.

_____

_____

_____

_____

_____

_____

6 There are mistakes in five of the following sentences. Find the mistakes and correct them.

a) Sea levels are likely ⁀to rise by over a metre by the end of the 21ˢᵗ century.

b) There well may be more electric cars than traditional petrol fuelled cars on our roads in as little as five years.

c) In ten years' time we could easily be using our body heat to recharge our mobile phones.

d) With new advances in nanotechnology, cancer and tumours will certainly almost become a thing of the past.

e) Bicycle sharing schemes could easily become compulsory in most European cities.

f) Scientists are bound to discovering a cure for Alzheimer's disease by the end of the century.

g) Human beings won't definitely ever be able to live to more than 120.

h) Power cuts and fuel shortages could easily become a part of day to day life as supplies of fossil fuels dwindle.

Look at the sentences again. Which predictions do you think are a) probable b) highly unlikely?

7 Complete the sentences with the expressions in the box so they reflect what you believe and feel about the future. Do not use any expression more than once.

will almost certainly   definitely won't
probably won't   might well   should
couldn't possibly   may possibly
is/are sure to   is/are unlikely to

a) My children's generation _____ have an easier life.

b) Advances in technology _____ reverse the process of climate change.

c) In ten years' time I _____ working a seven day week.

d) Digital texts _____ take the place of paper books.

e) Water _____ become more precious than oil.

f) A viable alternative for fossil fuels _____ be found in the next twenty years.

g) My generation _____ live to over a 120 years old.

h) I _____ have to move abroad to find a job in the next few years.

Vocabulary

1 Match words from box A with words from box B and label the objects below.

A

card	~~central~~	ear	evening	key
key	remote	touch	voice	wrist

B

band	board	mail	control	~~heating~~
meal	pad	piece	reader	screen

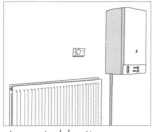

a) _central heating_

b) _____

c) _____

d) _____

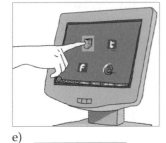

e) _____

f) _____

g) _____

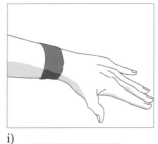

h) _____

i) _____

j) _____

2 Complete the compound nouns. Use one word only in each gap.

a) This revolutionary communication d_evice_ will soon make mobile phones a thing of the past.

b) He lives in a really remote area. It's a real 'not spot', there's no wifi and no cellular c_____ . You're totally cut off from the world up there!

c) They have a very extensive data n_____ with information on all public transport schedules across the country.

d) The local bus companies have just introduced a new payment s_____ that allows you to use your mobile phone credit to buy a ticket.

e) The offices are wired up to a security system that sends a remote a_____ to the local police station.

f) I wish people would send me a text when they can't get through on the mobile. I hate having to check my v_____ !

g) Have you been round to Tom's? He's got this amazing home e_____ system with a flat screen that hooks up directly to his netbook and plays movies and music directly off the internet.

h) I find grocery s_____ such a drag. I hate the queues in the supermarket, and I always end up buying a load of stuff I really don't need.

i) New speech r_____ software will mean that you can talk to your computer, but only if you have an American accent!

I say, old fellow, would you mind terribly printing that off for me again please. —thanks awfully

HEY..DUDE..WHAT.. LANGUAGE..YOU.. SPEAKING'..

3 Underline the correct word or expression.

a) The audience were well and truly **hyped / <u>wowed</u>** by the special effects.

b) Did you know that millions of mobile phones are **slick / trashed** every year?

c) There was a delay of over a year a half before the TV channel finally **sold on the idea / went digital.**

d) The presentation of the new prototype was very **slick / wow** and impressive.

e) As soon as he saw the sales figures he was completely **sold on the idea / trashed**!

f) There was so much **hype / slick** when the film first came out that it was very difficult for it to live up to expectations.

4 Use words or expressions from Exercise 3 to complete the texts below.

There's no such thing as bad publicity, or so the saying goes, but sometimes too much (1) _____ can backfire. Take a recent 'revolutionary' invention which claimed in its pre-launch publicity that it would profoundly affect the way people lived. The speculation reached dizzying heights and everybody was getting ready to be (2) _____ by a must-have device which would change all our lives overnight. Imagine the disappointment when it turned out to be nothing more than a low energy scooter!

Do you know, that man could sell ice to Eskimos! His presentation was so (3) _____ and clever. Not too overstated, not too loud or brash, he pitched it just right for his audience, and we were all totally (4) _____ . I signed up straight away!

As more and more schools and colleges prepare to (5) _____ , traditional textbook writers and publishers are worried. Is this the end of paper books, will all those much thumbed, much loved textbooks now just be (6) _____ ? Will we all convert to etextbooks brought to us on our mobile phones and ereaders?

5 Complete the sentences using one word in each gap.

a) What's all the soul searching about? It's not such a big ___*deal*___ you know. And hey, if you make the wrong decision, you can always change your mind.

b) Listen, I've thought it _____ really carefully, and I've decided that the answer is going to have to be no. I'm sorry!

c) Don't rush things, take your time, this is a really important decision, and remember, once you've taken it, there's no going _____ .

d) Stop dwelling on it. There's nothing you can do to change the past. What's _____ is _____ . Forget it and move on.

e) Now I know I've asked you this before, but are you sure you've thought through all the _____ consequences?

f) It's no good, I just keep going _____ and _____ in circles. I'm never going to be able to make up my mind.

g) Why don't you _____ on it and let me know in the morning?

h) Come on, what's with the long face? It isn't the _____ of the world, is it?

🌐 **26 Listen and check.**

Pronunciation

1 🌐 **27 Listen and underline the stressed part of the compound nouns in bold.**

a) Can I borrow your **mobile <u>phone</u>**?

b) Where's the **remote control** for the TV?

c) Have you had a look at the **travel schedule** yet? It's a killer!

d) It's a bit cold. Do you mind if I turn up the **central heating**?

e) I love these **touch screen** phones, but they're really difficult to keep clean.

f) That's a really pretty **wristband**. Where did you get it?

2 🌐 **28 Listen again and repeat the sentences.**

Reading

1 🌐 29 Read the news story below and explain the link between the story and the pictures 1–4.

a) The first image shows a man wearing an

_____ .

b) The second image shows _____
using the new discovery to _____

_____ .

c) The third image shows _____
using the new discovery to _____ .

d) The fourth image seems to show _____ ,
but there is actually a _____
which allows people behind the wall to _____

_____ .

2 Read the text again and answer the questions.

a) What new scientific development has been announced at St Andrews university?

b) How does it work?

c) What does the reporter compare it to?

d) What other similar development does the reporter describe?

e) Where and when was the second device first developed?

f) Which use has been criticised by human rights groups?

g) What are scientists worried about?

3 Find words in the text that mean:

a) presented (paragraph 1)

b) hides (paragraph 1)

c) an image whose the outline is not clear (paragraph 1)

d) an optical effect, common in deserts, whereby you think you can see something that isn't actually there (paragraph 1)

e) something that looks very different from what it actually is (paragraph 3)

f) an exclamation used to say that something happens suddenly as if by magic (paragraph 4)

g) to make something illegal (paragraph 4)

Presenting the invisible man!

Science fiction finally became fact as researchers at St Andrew's University today unveiled their controversial new invisibility cloak. Scientists in universities in the UK, USA, India and Japan have been working hard to develop a new type of metamaterial that can bend light, making the object it shields appear totally transparent. And the result is truly spectacular. What the eye sees is a strange fuzziness, not unlike heat haze on a distant road on a hot summer's day, or a mirage in the desert. So far, the largest object they have managed to cloak has been a small box, but the results are truly amazing. As the scientists lowered the cloak over the box, the box disappeared in front of our very eyes. It felt like some kind of magic trick. We were expecting someone to produce it suddenly from inside their sleeve or a top hat. Instead the cloak was raised, and the box reappeared.

The technology behind the cloak is complex and has taken many, many years of research. The key is in the structure of the metamaterial which is made up of tiny cone-like shapes that bend light around them instead of reflecting it as normal materials do.

This is different to virtual invisibility – or optical camouflage as it is otherwise known – which became a scientific fact back in 2003 when Japanese researchers developed an invisibility coat, a supposedly normal, green-grey rain coat, which was actually a screen that could project real-time images from behind the person wearing it, making it appear as if the person (or at least their coat) were invisible. This of course was simply a highly sophisticated special effect, an optical illusion, but it has proved very effective as a tool for surgeons, who can make their hands transparent in order to see the patient they are operating on,

or for airline pilots, who project images onto the floor of the cockpit in order to land more safely.

The screen has also been used to substitute for windows. The cloak, or screen, hangs on the wall on the inside of a building, the camera is positioned outside, and hey presto, the people on the inside can watch what's happening on the outside – without being observed. This last use of the technology has been criticised by human rights groups, who are trying to outlaw its use by police.

If the virtual invisibility cloak gives cause for concern, this second discovery, of a real invisibility cloak which could hide people, vehicles and even buildings, is sure to worry both human rights groups and governments. In fact scientists in the UK are already calling for government bodies to look into the possible future legal and security implications of this exciting, but worrying, invention.

Writing

Writing a discursive essay
Writing an introduction
Using discourse markers

1 **Which of the following things might you expect to see in the introduction to an essay?**

a) An introduction to the topic, demonstrating why the topic area is worth considering

b) Some of your arguments

c) Your general opinion

d) A basic repetition of the question

e) Evidence to support your arguments

f) A preview of your conclusion

g) A list of detailed examples

h) An outline of what you plan to say

2 **Read two introductions to two essays which are answering the same question. What is the question?**

a) Who was the greatest inventor of the 20th century?

b) Which was the most important discovery of the last fifty years?

c) What do you consider to be the most important invention of modern times?

3 **Read the two introductions again and decide which one is the best. Use your answers to Exercise 1 to help you.**

a Nowadays, the internet plays a major role in many areas of our society. However I don't think it is as important as the camera. When we started using the camera we completely changed our way of recording the past. Nowadays nearly all families have got digital cameras and camcorders – or use the same applications on their mobile phones – and use them to record weddings, anniversaries and special moments in their day to day lives. Before the camera, people had to record the past with paintings and so that is why there are far fewer records of the period before the camera was invented.

b Many people, looking back over the last part of the 20th century, claim that the internet has had a bigger impact on our lives than any other recent invention. I believe this to be a rather short-sighted view of our history. The car, the telephone and the television have all played a significant role in shaping our society. But when it comes to helping us record our past, I strongly believe there is only one candidate, the camera.

4 **Complete the text with some of the discourse markers in the box.**

for the first time	but then	prior to
not only	in this sense	it also meant that
but with	as well as	

(1) _____ did the camera change the way we record history, (2) _____ people from all walks of life could participate in creating historical documents for future generations. (3) _____ the invention of the camera, nearly all visual recollections of the past were in the form of paintings and drawings, which tended to be commissioned by the nobility or for religion. There were far fewer documents of how normal life was lived. (4) _____ the introduction of the camera, this all changed. (5) _____ people from all areas of life were able to document their lives.

5 **Choose an invention and write three reasons why you think it is the greatest invention of modern times.**

Invention _____

Reasons why

1 _____

2 _____

3 _____

6 **Write an essay which answers this question, using discourse markers from Exercise 4.**

'What do you consider to be the most important invention of modern times?'

You should write approximately 250 words.

Grammar

1 Complete the second sentence so it has the same meaning as the first sentence.

a) Katie Brown was listening to the radio in her kitchen when she heard that the radio station was giving away free sports cars.

In her kitchen, listening *to the radio, Katie heard that the radio station was giving away free sports cars.*

b) To win a sports car you had to answer three simple questions.

What you had _____

_____

c) Katie put down the potatoes she was peeling and phoned the radio station.

Putting _____

_____

d) The DJ read out the three questions and Katie answered them correctly.

The three questions _____

_____

e) When she went to the radio station to collect her prize, the DJ handed her a 10cm model of a sports car.

What the DJ _____

_____

_____

f) Katie was furious and decided to sue the radio station.

Furious, _____

_____

g) The court ruled in her favour and ordered the radio station to pay Katie £40,000 for the real car.

Ruling _____

_____

2 Complete the dialogue with an appropriate modal verb. Sometimes there is more than one possible answer.

Glen: Hi, Alan, you know that money I lent Giles? Well, he promised he (1) ____*would*____ pay back the loan within three weeks, but he (2) _____ have forgotten.

Alan: Well, didn't I warn you not to trust him? You (3) _____ have made him write you out a cheque, then you (4) _____ have avoided all these problems.

Glen: Well, you never know, he (5) _____ have genuinely forgotten.

Alan: Well, I think it's more likely that it's slipped his mind because it suits him. Anyway, didn't he say he (6) _____ come over to see us this weekend? Well, where is he?

Glen: Yes, you're right. I (7) _____ to have insisted that he gave me a cheque.

🌀 30 **Listen and check.**

3 Each of the following sentences has one word missing. Insert the missing word.

a) She promised she ˌ*would*ˌ phone if there were any problems.

b) I'm really sorry, I have been looking where I was going.

c) I know I really ought have phoned sooner, but I was terribly busy.

d) His phone was engaged. I suppose he might have talking to his sister.

e) I thought he'd have arrived by now – he must got stuck in the traffic.

f) Why's the light still on? You should been asleep by now!

g) You should have told me there was no food in the house – I have gone to the shops.

h) I'm sorry, I really don't know where it is – I suppose might have left it at home.

4 Rewrite the following sentences using the modal verb in brackets.

a) He's over an hour late. The only possible explanation is that he's forgotten about the appointment. (must)

He's over an hour later. He must have forgotten about the appointment.

b) 'I really can't afford to buy a new car, it's far too expensive,' he explained. (could)

_____

_____

c) She believes it was possibly intentional. (might)

_____

_____

d) I told you to get the boiler checked. Now it doesn't work, it's freezing and it's the middle of winter. (should)

_____

_____

e) 'I'll make sure all the doors are locked and all the lights switched off,' Cathy promised. (would)

_____

_____

f) They can't be the ones who stole the money, they didn't have enough time. (could)

_____

_____

g) I'm sure he didn't know about your news, or he'd have said something. (can)

_____

_____

h) I'm disappointed that you didn't let us know you were coming to town last weekend. (could)

_____

_____

i) I really don't know what I did with my sunglasses. I suppose it's possible that I left them at the restaurant. (may)

_____

_____

j) Cara used to be a terrible time-keeper when she was younger. She always turned up late for everything. (would)

_____

_____

5 Match the beginnings of the sentences (*a–g*) with their endings (*1–7*).

a) He was so disappointed with the outcome of the court case
b) She wasn't expecting to get the job
c) He hates the fact that he has to work on the night shift
d) There was such confusion over the new voting system
e) He has such a bad reputation for not paying his debts
f) She wasn't happy to help
g) They were so surprised when he told them that he'd passed his exam

1 that no one will lend him any money.
2 and his wife, who has to spend the evenings alone, does too.
3 that they could hardly believe him.
4 and she wasn't willing to say why.
5 and she certainly didn't expect to be offered such a generous salary.
6 that he decided to give up practising law.
7 that many people voted for the wrong candidate.

a	b	c	d	e	f	g
6						

6 Rewrite the sentences in Exercise 5 beginning with the words given below:

a) So disappointed *was he with the outcome of the court case that he decided to give up practising law.*

b) She wasn't expecting to get the job, nor _____

_____

_____

c) He hates the fact that he has to work on the night shift and so _____

_____

_____

d) Such was _____

_____

e) So bad _____

_____

f) She was neither _____

nor _____

g) Such was _____

_____

_____

Vocabulary

1 Choose the correct answer.

a) Which of these punishments would a judge probably not give in court?

   1 suspended sentence   2 <u>solitary confinement</u>
   3 community service

b) Which one of these crimes involves fire?

   1 arson   2 embezzlement
   3 speeding

c) Which one of these is the least serious crime?

   1 manslaughter   2 speeding
   3 libel

d) Which of these is not a lawyer?

   1 attorney   2 barrister
   3 the accused

e) Which of the following does the judge not do?

   1 award damages   2 cross examine
   3 sentence

f) Which of the following does the jury not do?

   1 return a verdict   2 weigh up the evidence
   3 sue

2 Use words and phrases from Exercise 1 to complete the sentences below.

a) When her company fired her with no advance notice, Clare decided to _____*sue*_____ them for damages.

b) It was the worst case of _____ that the fire service had ever seen.

c) _____ bowed her head and cried as the sentence against her was read out to the court.

d) The judge sentenced the two teenage boys to eight months of _____ , stressing that he hoped that helping others would help them see the error of their ways.

e) The counsel for the defence stood up to _____ the witness, but said he had no questions to ask.

f) The case was so straightforward, the jury took only 30 minutes to _____ of guilty.

g) It was the third time he'd been stopped for _____ – and on the same stretch of road!

h) The newspaper was cleared of all charges of _____ on the grounds that the story they had previously reported had since been shown to be true.

3 Complete these expressions to do with law with the words in the box.

above   against   by   down
into   is   ~~unto~~   with

a) a law ____*unto*____ himself

b) lay _____ the law

c) taking the law _____ your own hands

d) no-one is _____ the law

e) in trouble _____ the law

f) his word _____ law

g) _____ law

h) _____ the law

4 Choose the most appropriate expressions from Exercise 3 to complete the sentences below.

a) It's up to the police to control crime. There's no point in _____ .

b) The police are always going round to his parents' house. He's constantly _____ _____ .

c) Her father really used to _____ _____ . He would order her to be home by 11 pm.

d) He acts as if he were _____ and can get away with anything, but one day he'll find himself in big trouble.

e) You can never tell how Tony's going to react. He's _____ .

f) The playing of music on the underground is prohibited _____ unless you have a licence.

g) It is _____ to drive a motorbike without wearing a helmet.

h) When it comes to a final decision, Jason's _____ and no-one can contradict him.

5 Match the formal words (*a–h*) to their more neutral forms (*1–8*).

a) prior to   1 start
b) prominent   2 very bad
c) seek   3 in addition
d) severe   4 before
e) further   5 well-known
f) depict   6 later
g) commence   7 ask for
h) in due course   8 show

a	b	c	d	e	f	g	h
4							

6 Use the words and phrases *a–h* in Exercise 5 to complete the following extracts from news reports. Make any necessary changes.

a

A ___prominent___ barrister has been brought to trial for negligence. A former client is _____ compensation for damages to his image.

b

The court case against football star, Rick Hughes, is due to _____ this week. Hughes has been charged with inflicting _____ injuries on a fan who invaded the pitch during a league game last season.

c

Part of the exhibition consisted of photos _____ the town centre _____ the devastating earthquake.

d

The new high speed train service in Scotland will be considerably more expensive than the present service. _____ , it will only be available along the east coast, although there are plans to extend the service towards the west and the highlands _____ .

7 Complete the exclamations with one word. The first letter has been given to you.

a) Did I h*ear*_____ you right? They're going to arrest him?

b) Come on, you've g_____ to be kidding! She'd never do anything like that, surely!

c) You don't e_____ me to believe that do you? I've never heard such nonsense in all my life!

d) Well I n_____ ! Who'd have t_____ it! She really is a dark horse, isn't she?

e) Why not? You never can t_____ . Dave's always known how to surprise us.

f) No! That c_____ be right! He'd have told me.

g) Promotion? No k_____ ! I thought she was thinking about resigning.

h) Lola's going to take the whole team out for a meal? Hm, I'll b_____ that when I see it.

8 Write the words in the correct order to form common idiomatic expressions associated with surprise and disbelief.

a) fly   and   might   pigs   !

_____

b) book   can't   you   cover   judge   by   a   its

_____

c) waters   deep   still   run

_____

d) one   other   pull   the   !

_____

9 Match the idioms (*a–d*) in Exercise 8 to their meanings (*1–4*).

1   Used for saying that people who are shy or who do not say much often have very strong feelings or interesting ideas. ☐

2   Used for saying you don't believe what someone is saying to you. ☐

3   Used for saying you shouldn't form an opinion about someone or something only from their appearance. ☐

4   Used for saying something is completely impossible. ☐

Pronunciation

🌐 **31 Listen to these people expressing surprise. Look at the words in bold and think about whether the speaker's voice is high or low, and rising or falling.**

a)   **No**! You must be **joking**!

b)   **Never**! Pull the other one, it's got bells on it!

c)   You did **what**? I can't **believe** it!

d)   **Who** did you say? **Martin**? That just **can't** be right.

e)   **Really**? The **two** of them? But **when**?

f)   Well, **who**'d have thought it. What a **dark** horse!

Listen again and repeat.

Listening

1 ● 32 **Cover the script and listen to two friends, Alistair and Sarita, discussing the problems involved in doing jury service. Make a note of what they think is:**

a) the main problem

_____

_____

b) a possible benefit of doing jury service

_____

_____

2 **Listen again and decide if the statements below are true (*T*) or false (*F*).**

a) Neither speaker has done any jury service. ☐

b) They have both been reading the same article in the newspaper. ☐

c) Some employers refuse to give their employees permission to do jury service. ☐

d) Jurors are paid their normal wage during jury service. ☐

e) Most people are happy to do jury service. ☐

f) Some cases can last a long time. ☐

g) Sometimes jurors are not allowed to see their families during jury service. ☐

h) Elena is interested in doing jury service. ☐

3 **Complete these extracts from the conversation with an appropriate preposition.**

a) … more and more people are trying to get _____ of it if they can.

b) … there's a problem about taking time _____.

c) … they don't actually have to pay your wages when you're _____ jury service …

d) … it's much less than most people earn _____ work …

e) I mean it sounds like a good thing to do _____ theory …

f) … but if you're going to be _____ of pocket …

g) … that seems to be what's _____ the root of the problem.

h) … you might be called to sit _____ a simple case

i) … the jury have to be isolated _____ the press

Listen again and check.

Alistair	Have you ever done any jury service?
Sarita	No, I haven't. Why are you asking?
Alistair	Oh, nothing … just that I've been reading this thing in the paper about how more and more people are trying to get out of it if they can.
Sarita	Really? I'd have thought it'd be quite interesting.
Alistair	Yeah, so would I, but it seems that there's a problem about taking time off work.
Sarita	Yeah? What, like their bosses won't give them time off?
Alistair	No, no, that's not the problem, I mean your employer has to let you off. I mean, they can't refuse to give you the time off. No, no, sometimes they might actually be really happy to let you off, you know, 'cos they don't actually have to pay your wages when you're on jury service.
Sarita	Are you sure? That seems very strange.
Alistair	Well, I think it's true, that's what it says here anyway.
Sarita	But if you're not being paid … I mean that's hardly very fair, is it?
Alistair	I think you get some kind of allowance … you know, the court give you like a daily allowance whilst you're on jury service.
Sarita	That sounds more like it. I mean, they can't force you to do something without offering some compensation.
Alistair	Yeah, but apparently it's not a lot … I mean, it's much less than most people earn at work, so lots of jurors are doing everything they can to get out of doing their stint.
Sarita	Mmm, yeah, I see … I think I would too … I mean, it sounds like a good thing to do in theory … you know, interesting to find out exactly how our system of justice works and all that, but if you're going to be out of pocket … well …
Alistair	Yeah, that seems to be what's at the root of the problem. That and the time it takes sometimes.
Sarita	What do you mean?
Alistair	Well, you might be called to sit on a simple case which only takes a matter of days, but some cases can go on for weeks … or months even.
Sarita	Yeah, and what about if you get called onto some high profile case … you know something that's in the news. The pressure must be really tough.
Alistair	Yeah, the jury have to be isolated from the press … sometimes they can't even speak to their own families.
Sarita	Well, in that case, I think I'd try to wriggle out of it too!

Writing

Writing a short report
Reporting statistics

1 Read the report and choose the best title.

   a) One in five youngsters are criminals.

   b) Youth crime is on the increase.

   c) Loss of jobs main factor in increased youth crime.

2 Read it again and complete the text with the words and phrases in the box.

> an average   compared with   ~~figures~~
>
> more likely   over a quarter   than by those
>
> the vast majority   was found

(1) _____*Figures*_____ in this year's annual crime report show that more than 20% of young people between the ages of 10 and 25 committed at least one crime during the last 12 months. (2) _____ (28%) of these offenders admitted to committing six or more crimes.

    Boys are (3) _____ to have offended than girls, with 31% of boys admitting to offences (4) _____ 18% of girls.

    More crimes were committed by young offenders under 18 (5) _____ between 18 and 25. The peak age for offending (6) _____ to be 13–16, especially among boys.

    It is no surprise, however, that (7) _____ of young offenders (more than 80%) under the age of 16 were also truants, missing (8) _____ of 25–30 days of school a year.

    Police representatives have once again stressed that the only way to fight youth crime is to keep young people in education.

3 Look at the figures and information in the charts opposite and complete the sentences.

   a) _____ % of men who go to prison for 12 months re-offend within 12 months.

   b) _____ % of women who go to prison for 12 months re-offend within 12 months.

   c) The commonest crime for re-offenders is _____ .

   d) _____ account for 18% of crimes by re-offenders.

   e) Ex-prisoners often re-offend because they cannot get a _____ .

   f) Amongst prisoners who go on job training programmes, _____ % do not find work when they are released.

   g) Amongst prisoners who find _____ _____ , 80% do not re-offend.

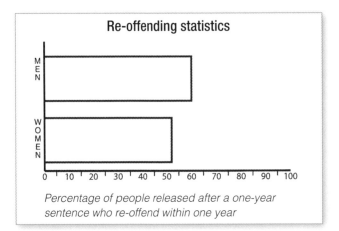

Re-offending statistics

Percentage of people released after a one-year sentence who re-offend within one year

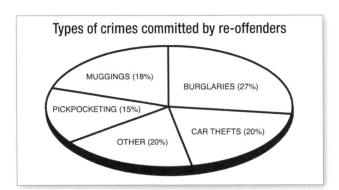

Types of crimes committed by re-offenders

MUGGINGS (18%)   BURGLARIES (27%)   PICKPOCKETING (15%)   OTHER (20%)   CAR THEFTS (20%)

REASONS FOR RE-OFFENDING: No possibility of getting a job, boredom, lack of money.

TRAINING: of prisoners who receive job training (e.g. IT or construction), 60% find work when released.

EMPLOYMENT: Only 20% of ex-prisoners who find stable employment re-offend.

4 Write a report based on the figures in Exercise 3. Start with a brief introduction and then cover the following points in whatever order seems best to you. It should be no longer than 250 words.

- the percentage of re-offenders amongst men and women
- reasons why people re-offend
- a suggestion of what the government could do to help reduce the figures
- the types of crime they commit when they re-offend

Night

Grammar

1 Underline the correct alternative.

a. The average adult needs about eight hours sleep a night. Some studies, **however / yet / although**, suggest that women need an hour more sleep than men.

b. Eating a meal just before bed is not recommended. Eating a small snack, **yet / though / although**, can actually help you sleep.

c. Men tend to dream more about men, **however / but / even though** women, according to research, dream equally about men and women.

d. We very often dream about ourselves, **despite / although / however** this doesn't start happening until we are about five years old.

e. Sleepwalkers are technically asleep **even so / even though / despite** they have their eyes open and sometimes even engage in conversation.

f. Some animals such as cows and elephants can sleep standing up. They can only dream when they are lying down, **yet / even so / however**.

g. **Even though / Despite / However** many years of research, it is still not known whether fish sleep at all.

h. Everyone knows the expression 'thinking on your feet', **yet / although / even so** studies have shown that on average we think 10% faster when we are lying down.

2 Complete the news items with the words in the boxes.

| but | despite | ~~even though~~ | though |

CONSIDERATE CAR THIEF

Joe Davis of Miami is still furious, (1) _even though_ the thief that rifled through his car and took his CDs, cash, driver's license and credit cards left a nice note behind.

The note read: *'You have amazing taste in music. Don't worry about your credit cards and driver's license – I know I can't use them … after tonight, at least. Seriously (2) _____, lock your car in the future.'*

The note was handwritten and signed 'P' but (3) _____ the thief's audacity, his or her identity remains unknown.

Police say that a thief leaving a note is rare, (4) _____ that car burglaries are not.

| despite | even though | however |
| nevertheless | yet | |

FAKE PHONE FELONS

Employees at a mobile phone store arrived at work on Tuesday morning to find that the store had been broken into. (5) _____ , the only items missing were hollow replica display phones.

'(6) _____ they look real, they are completely worthless,' said store manager Eva Martinez. 'We've got hundreds of real phones on the premises (7) _____ the thieves just walked right past them. It's a mystery.'

(8) _____ the minimal loss, the store owners (9) _____ reported the theft to local police, who are investigating.

| but | despite | however | that said |
| try as I might | | | |

THE CRATE ESCAPE

John Franklin, a cleaner from Illinois, decided last month to post himself to his best friend as a birthday surprise. He climbed into a large crate and got his wife to post him to his friend's house thirty miles away. (10) _____ , the crate went missing and (11) _____ Mr Franklin's shouts and frantic banging, his plight was not discovered for six days. '(12) _____ , I just couldn't get anyone's attention,' said Franklin. Postal workers recalled hearing faint banging noises, (13) _____ assumed it was the depot's heating system. Franklin's wife described her husband as 'stark raving mad'. '(14) _____ , I did get six days' break from his incessant pranks,' she added.

🔊 **33 Listen and check.**

3 Complete the sentences so they are true for you.

a) Try as I might, *I just can't stop eating chocolate.*

b) Strange as it may seem, _____
_____

c) _____ . That said,
_____

d) In spite of my efforts, _____
_____

e) Try as I might, _____
_____

4 What are the people thinking? Use words from each box in the correct form.

| book | go | not go | not steal | ~~work~~ |

| to bed earlier | ~~harder~~ | to the hairdresser's |
| that car | in advance |

a) I so wish _I'd worked_
harder.

b) If only _____
_____

c) I wish _____
_____

d) I really regret _____
_____

e) If only _____

5 Freddie went to a party last night. Rewrite his regrets beginning with the words in brackets.

a) Why on earth did I drink so much? (really wish)

I really wish I hadn't drunk so much.

b) I shouldn't have eaten so much. (really regret)

_____

c) I can't believe I danced with Anna! (wish)

_____

d) It's a pity I didn't get to speak to Katie. (If only)

_____

e) I sang 'I will survive' at karaoke! (so wish)

_____

f) I made a fool of myself. (so regret)

_____

6 Complete these famous quotations about regret by putting the verb into the correct tense or form.

a) I regret ___not having had___ (not have) more time with my kids when they were growing up. (*Tina Turner, singer*)

b) I wish I _____ (invent) blue jeans. They have expression, modesty, sex appeal, simplicity – all I hope for in my clothes. (*Yves Saint Laurent, designer*)

c) If I _____ (know) I was going to live this long, I _____ (take) better care of myself. (*Eubie Blake, musician*)

d) I wish they _____ (have) electric guitars in cotton fields back in the good old days. A whole lot of things _____ (be) straightened out. (*Jimi Hendrix, musician*)

e) I have no regrets. I _____ (not live) my life the way I did if I _____ (go) to worry about what people were going to say. (*Ingrid Bergman, actress*)

7 Think of some regrets in your life. Write about them by completing the sentences below.

a) It's a real pity _____
_____

b) I really regret _____
_____

c) If only _____
_____

d) I'd have liked _____
_____

Pronunciation

1 🌐 34 In speech *had, would* and *have* are often contracted. Listen to how they are pronounced in these sentences.

a) I wish you <u>had</u> been there.

b) If you <u>had</u> been there, you <u>would</u> <u>have</u> had a great time.

2 How would the following sentences sound with *had, would* and *have* contracted?

a) If only I had gone out last night.

b) I wish I had had more time.

c) If you had been there, you would have loved it.

d) I would like to have gone with you.

e) Peter would have loved it too.

🌐 35 Listen and check. Repeat the sentences.

Night   UNIT **9**   **53**

Vocabulary

1 Find ten times of day in the puzzle. One has been done for you. The words go →, ↓ and ↘.

N	D	S	U	N	S	E	T	F
M	I	D	N	I	G	H	T	M
D	B	G	K	N	R	T	J	I
A	U	Y	H	S	O	Q	L	D
W	Z	S	H	T	P	O	H	D
N	B	X	K	Q	F	M	N	A
D	A	Y	B	R	E	A	K	Y
S	U	N	R	I	S	E	L	V
T	W	I	L	I	G	H	T	L

_____sunrise_____   _____

_____   _____

_____   _____

_____   _____

_____   _____

2 Complete these times of day by adding the missing letters.

a) the middle of the night

b) th_ w_ _ sm_ll h_ _rs

c) f_rst th_ng _n th_ m_rn_ng

d) l_st th_ng _t n_ght

e) th_ cr_ck _f d_wn

f) m_d - _ft_rn_ _ n

3 Complete the sentences with the times of day in Exercise 2.

a) Sam phoned me from Australia in _the middle of the night_ last night. I think it was about three-thirty. He'd forgotten about the time difference!

b) I've been waking up at _____ lately. I think it's the sun coming through the curtains that's waking me up.

c) We'll try and set off _____ . We'll have lunch and then pack, so I guess about three-ish.

d) We stayed up chatting into _____ last night. I think it was about two when we finally went to bed.

e) I like to read in bed for half an hour _____ . It helps me get to sleep.

f) I'll call you _____ . What time do you get up?

4 Complete the descriptions with the words phrases and phrases in the box.

> all night long   early night   ~~hen night~~
> nightcap   nightlife   night on the town
> overnight   stag night

a) They're on a ____hen____ _night_

b) They're on a _____ _____

c) There's lots of _____ _____

d) It's an _____ flight.

e) They're having a _____

f) He's been working _____

g) They're having a _____

h) She's having an _____

5 Underline the correct alternative.

a) It took me ages to **drop** _off_ / _out_ last night.

b) I like a glass wine at the end of the day to help me **wind** _away_ / _down_.

c) I couldn't get to sleep last night. I was still **totally** _groggy_ / _alert_ at two in the morning.

d) I was so tired last night I **slept like a** _tree_ / _log_.

e) I **went out like a** _light_ / _night_ last night.

f) The neighbours were having an all-night party last night. I **didn't get a** _nod_ / _wink_ **of sleep**.

g) I've always **been a** _light_ / _gentle_ **sleeper**. The slightest thing wakes me up.

h) I need a few days rest to **recharge my** _power_ / _batteries_.

6 Match the expressions in bold in Exercise 5 with expressions with a similar meaning (1–8).

1	relax	b
2	fall asleep	
3	slept soundly	
4	completely awake	
5	had a sleepless night	
6	fell asleep immediately	
7	renew my energy levels	
8	woken up easily when disturbed	

7 Put the words in italics into the correct order in these dialogues.

a) A: Are you doing anything tonight?

B: _have No, what did mind? in you_
<u>No, what did you have in mind?</u>

b) A: _to you What this evening? are up_
_____

B: Nothing special.

c) A: _drink you go a like 'd wondering I was if sometime? to for_
_____
_____

B: That sounds great! I'd love to!

d) A: Fancy coming over for a bite to eat tonight?

B: _tonight. going but out you, really That's kind of I'm_
_____
_____

e) A: Are you free on Thursday evening?

B: _'m on then. 've something I afraid got I_
_____

f) A: How about a game of tennis on Friday?

B: _Saturday. free make can't but I'm I Friday, on_
_____
_____

8 Complete the conversation with the words in the box.

> fancied   eyes   mind   shame   sounds
> sometime   time   ~~up~~   up

Alex: Hi Jim, it's Alex. What are you (1) ___up___ to tonight?

Jim: I'm pretty busy actually. I'm up to my (2) _____ with work at the moment.

Alex: Oh, that's a (3) _____ . I was wondering if you (4) _____ going for a drink?

Jim: I'd love to, but as I said, I'm really tied (5) _____ . Some other (6) _____ perhaps.

Alex: OK, never (7) _____ . Maybe (8) _____ next week?

Jim: Yes, that (9) _____ good.

> about   along   could   fancies   good
> make   say   then   to

Alex: How (10) _____ Monday or Tuesday?

Jim: Tuesday sounds (11) _____ . We (12) _____ check out that new bar on Ship Street.

Alex: OK. I hear it's pretty good. Eight thirty?

Jim: Fine. Actually, could we (13) _____ it a bit later? (14) _____ , nine thirty? I've got my sister over for dinner.

Alex: Fine. Why don't you bring her (15) _____ ? I haven't seen her for years.

Jim: OK, I'll see if she (16) _____ it.

Alex: Great, half nine on Tuesday (17) _____ .

Jim: OK, looking forward (18) _____ it.

Alex: See you. Bye.

Jim: Bye.

🌐 **36 Listen and check.**

Reading

Why do we sleep?

Every animal does it and humans on average need between six and nine hours of it each day. And if we don't get enough of it, we suffer the disruptive effects of deprivation such as the inability to perform mental and physical tasks. And yet, despite centuries of research into it and the existence of numerous theories, there is still no general consensus on why we do it.

One theory is that sleep enables the brain to 'take stock' of the day that has just finished and to organise and archive the information and the memories that arise from it. Dreams have long been thought of as a by-product of this process.

Another theory is that sleep provides a period of mental inactivity so that the brain can rest, recharge itself and recuperate; a kind of daily 'down time'.

The biological view is that sleep is the time when the body grows and repairs itself. Growth hormone is released when we sleep and proteins, the body's building blocks, are created at night. Studies have shown that growth in children can be stunted by sleep deprivation and in adults, insufficient sleep increases susceptibility to disease.

However, while there is still possibly some truth in all these theories, there may be a rather more prosaic explanation for why sleep evolved. It is thought that our ancestors slept simply because at night they couldn't see and couldn't do anything to sustain themselves. In other words, there was nothing for them to do and it made sense for them to use this time to rest and conserve energy.

While experts can't agree on why we sleep, the cause of sleep is not disputed. A chemical called adenosine builds up with brain activity during the day and it is believed that once a certain concentration is reached, the chemical begins to 'shut off' connections in the brain, making us feel tired. The more brain activity there is during the day, the more adenosine is produced and the tireder we get.

1 🌐 37 Read the text. Which two of the following are **not** mentioned as a reason why we sleep?

a) to enable the brain to organise information

b) to allow the brain to rest and recover

c) because there is too much demand on the brain at night

d) to allow muscles and other tissue to rest

e) allow the body to grow and repair itself

f) because there is nothing to do at night

2 Read these statements and decide if they are true (*T*) or false (*F*) according to the text.

a) All animals sleep. ☐

b) Experts know why we sleep. ☐

c) Body growth occurs at night. ☐

d) Children who get too much sleep can have growth problems. ☐

e) Adults who do not get enough sleep are more likely to get ill. ☐

f) Our ancestors had no reason to be awake at night. ☐

g) The chemical adenosine is produced when we sleep. ☐

h) The level of adenosine in the body is related to how tired we feel. ☐

3 Find a word in the text which means:

a) causing difficulties (paragraph 1)

b) not having what you need (paragraph 1)

c) agreement among all people (paragraph 1)

d) spend time thinking about what has happened (paragraph 2)

e) recover (paragraph 3)

f) a time when someone or a machine is not working (paragraph 3)

g) prevented from growing correctly (paragraph 4)

h) likelihood of being affected (paragraph 4)

i) ordinary, lacking excitement (paragraph 5)

j) argued about (paragraph 6)

4 What do you think the text is?

a) a news article

b) a letter from a doctor

c) the abstract of an academic paper

d) a student essay for school or university

Writing

1 Look at the essay 'Why do we sleep?' on page 56 and do the following tasks.

    a) Number the following sections in the order in which they occur in the essay:

       Summary of research to date ☐

       What experts agree on ☐

       Background ☐

       The theories ☐

    b) Find an example of where research is mentioned to support a theory.

       _____

    c) What two other words are used instead of 'theory' in paragraphs 4 and 5.

       _____

    d) Find five concessive discourse markers.

       _____

       _____

2 Complete the sentences with the words in the box. Use each word or phrase once.

> another theory   despite   however
>
> one theory   while   yet

    a) We all need sleep, _____ no-one knows precisely why we need it.

    b) _____ many years of research, there is no consensus.

    c) _____ is that sleep enables the brain to organise information.

    d) _____ is that sleep allows the brain a period of rest.

    e) Some people can survive on just four hours sleep a night. _____ , most people need between six and nine hours a night.

    f) _____ experts agree on the chemical cause of sleep, their opinions differ when it comes to why we sleep.

3 You are going to write an essay that answers the question 'Why do we dream?'.

- Use some or all of the notes below for your essay. Add any other information you like.
- Plan the order and the content of the paragraphs.
- Think about how to expand the notes into complete sentences, and how to connect the sentences and paragraphs.
- Try to use concessive and other discourse markers.
- Write your essay. You should write about 250 words.

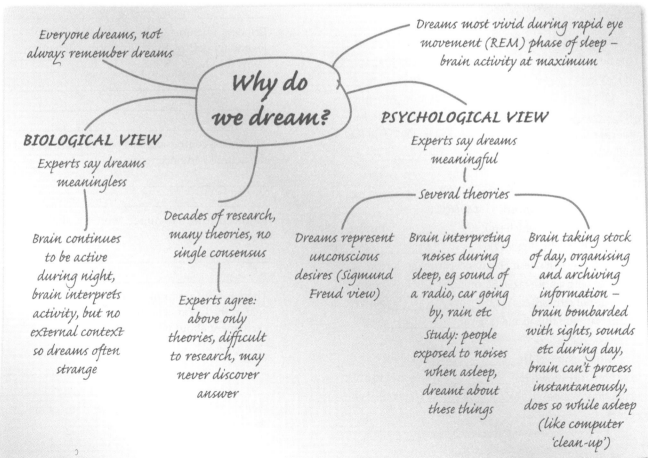

Everyone dreams, not always remember dreams

Dreams most vivid during rapid eye movement (REM) phase of sleep – brain activity at maximum

Why do we dream?

BIOLOGICAL VIEW

Experts say dreams meaningless

PSYCHOLOGICAL VIEW

Experts say dreams meaningful

Several theories

Brain continues to be active during night, brain interprets activity, but no external context so dreams often strange

Decades of research, many theories, no single consensus

Experts agree: above only theories, difficult to research, may never discover answer

Dreams represent unconscious desires (Sigmund Freud view)

Brain interpreting noises during sleep, eg sound of a radio, car going by, rain etc

Study: people exposed to noises when asleep, dreamt about these things

Brain taking stock of day, organising and archiving information – brain bombarded with sights, sounds etc during day, brain can't process instantaneously, does so while asleep (like computer 'clean-up')

10 Footprints

Grammar

1 Complete the article by putting the verb into the correct passive form. You do not need to use the auxiliary verb *be* in some cases.

Famous shoes – Dorothy's ruby slippers

In the 1939 movie classic *The Wizard of Oz*, Dorothy (1) __is given__ (give) a pair of magical ruby slippers. In the original story, the shoes were silver, but they (2) _____ (change) to ruby red to take advantage of the new Technicolor film process. The shoes have become one of the most iconic images from the film.

It (3) _____ (believe) that seven pairs of Dorothy's red slippers (4) _____ (create) for the film. Today, the whereabouts of only four pairs (5) _____ (know).

One pair is in the Smithsonian Institution, two others (6) _____ (own) by private collectors, and a fourth pair (7) _____ (steal) in 2005 from the Judy Garland Museum and (8) _____ (yet/be) recovered.

The last pair to come up for sale (9) _____ (sell) at auction by Christie's for $666,000.

A pair of shoes which (10) _____ (inspire) by Dorothy's ruby slippers (11) _____ (recently/put) on sale at Harrods department store in London with a price tag of £2 million.

The red satin stilettos (12) _____ (weave) from platinum thread and (13) _____ (set) with 642 rubies.

After pictures (14) _____ (take) for the press, the shoes (15) _____ (place) in a bulletproof case and (16) _____ (guard) at all times.

🔊 38 **Listen and check.**

2 Rewrite the sentences using the passive form of the verbs. Omit the agent if this is not known, irrelevant or obvious.

The world's most expensive shoes

a) American designer Stuart Weitzman made the world's most expensive shoes.

   The world's most expensive shoes were made by
   American designer Stuart Weitzman.

b) Experts value the shoes at $3 million.

   _____

c) Princess Yasmin Aga Khan, the daughter of legendary actress Rita Hayworth, currently owns the shoes.

   _____
   _____
   _____

d) The shoes' centrepiece is a pair of earrings that the actress had once worn.

   _____
   _____

e) Kathleen York, a nominee, wore the shoes at the Oscars in 2006.

   _____
   _____

f) There is now a pair of Weitzman shoes every year at the Oscars and there is always great excitement about who will wear them.

   _____
   _____
   _____

g) Weitzman has sold several other pairs of his shoes for over $1 million.

   _____
   _____

3 Complete the text with the correct passive form of the verbs in the boxes. You do not need to use the auxiliary verb *be* in some cases.

| find | make | photograph | ~~ever take~~ |

This is one of the most famous photographs
(1) ___*ever taken*___ and shows what is perhaps the most famous footprint in history.

The footprint (2) _____ and
(3) _____ by Buzz Aldrin during NASA's 1969 Apollo 11 mission as part of an experiment to study the nature of lunar dust.
The dust (4) _____ to compact easily, leaving this iconic impression of the boot.

| not disturb | eventually erode | leave | make |

Because there is no weather on the Moon, Aldrin's footprint (5) _____ for millions of years until it (6) _____ by micrometeorite impacts.

Footprints (7) _____ on the moon by a total of twelve astronauts along with tyre tracks (8) _____ by the Lunar Rover vehicle in the later Apollo missions.

| give | finally discuss | predict | speak |

Aldrin was in fact the second man to walk on the moon, the honour of being the first
(9) _____ to Neil Armstrong, the mission commander. Aldrin, however, can claim the first words (10) _____ from the moon: 'Tranquility Base. The Eagle has landed.'

Today, over forty years later, the next generation of manned flights to the moon (11) _____
_____. And it (12) _____ that by 2030 there may even be human footprints on Mars.

4 Complete the sentences comparing the countries' ecological footprints. Use each word or phrase in the box once.

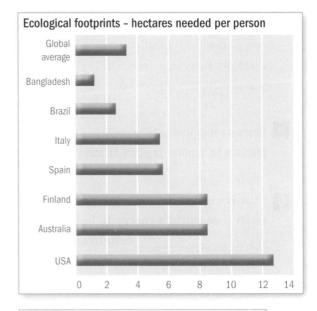

| by far | considerably | just | somewhat |
| nothing like | very slightly | | |

a) The USA's ecological footprint is
___*by far*___ the biggest of those shown.

b) Spain's ecological footprint is _____ bigger than Italy's.

c) Finland's footprint is _____ as big as Australia's.

d) Brazil's footprint is _____ less than the global average.

e) Bangladesh's footprint is _____ smaller than the other countries'.

f) The other countries' ecological footprints are _____ as big as the USA's.

5 Write sentences to show your own opinion. Use the words given and choose a word from the box.

| far | a lot | infinitely | much | way | a bit |
| a little | slightly | just | nowhere near | | |

a) football / rugby / exciting
   Rugby is far more exciting than football.

b) skiing / snowboarding / dangerous
   _____

c) Brad Pitt / Johnny Depp / good-looking
   _____

d) being happy / being rich / important
   _____

e) playing computer games / shopping / fun
   _____

f) writing English / speaking English / easy
   _____

Vocabulary

1 Complete the news headlines with the words in the box.

energy-efficient	~~locally-grown~~	
organic	recycled	renewable
solar-powered	sustainable	

a Restaurant to use only _____*locally grown*_____ produce to support region's farmers

b Massive investment in wind power as 50% of world's energy to be from _____ resources by 2050

c Not enough sun in UK for _____ cars say experts

d Sales of _____ produce falls during economic crisis

e New _____ washing machine to cost one cent per wash

f _____ tourism is only way to avoid loss of minority groups

g Glossy magazine industry urged to use _____ paper

2 Match the sentence beginnings (a–i) with their endings (1–9).

a) I put my   1 feet.
b) I've got itchy   2 foot down.
c) I've got a   3 foot in the door.
d) I waited on him   4 hand and foot.

a	b	c	d
2			

e) I put my   5 foot in it.
f) I need to stand on   6 feet.
g) I got cold   7 foot wrong.
h) I put my   8 feet up.
i) I didn't put a   9 my own two feet.

e	f	g	h	i

3 Find expressions in Exercise 2 that have similar meaning to the sentences.

a) I accidentally said the wrong thing. It was quite embarrassing.

_____

b) I've had enough of this place. I need to travel.

_____

c) I've been introduced to the boss of the company and he seems quite interested in me.

_____

d) I did absolutely everything for him.

_____

e) I very firmly said 'no'.

_____

f) I really must be more independent.

_____

g) I changed my mind at the last minute.

_____

h) I relaxed for a while.

_____

i) I didn't make a single mistake.

_____

4 Complete the crossword with the names of the different kinds of footwear.

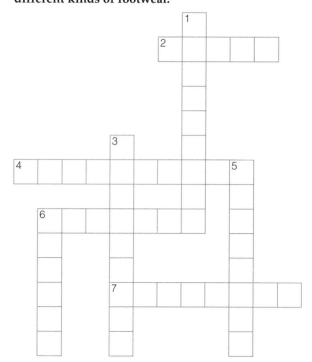

ACROSS

2

4

6

7

DOWN

1

3

5

6

5 Complete the dialogues with the words in the box.

arm	defeatist	do	gained	~~go~~
go	good	happy	know	point
twisted	ventured	want		

a) A: Do you think I ought to apply for the job?

    B: Yeah, I think you should ___*go*___ for it.

b) A: Aaarrgh! I'll never get it right!

    B: Don't be _____ ! Of course you will.

c) A: I'm sure I won't be able to sort the computer out myself.

    B: It's worth giving it a _____ .

d) A: I'm not sure about going out tonight. And I can't really afford it to be honest.

    B: Go on, it'll _____ you _____ .

e) A: I really shouldn't have a dessert. I'm trying to lose a few kilos.

    B: Go on, you _____ you _____ to really.

f) A: Come on, come with us.

    B: Oh alright, you've _____ my _____ .

g) A: I'd much rather go for a pizza. I'm not in the mood for an Indian.

    B: OK then, if it'll make you _____ .

h) A: You should talk to your boss if you're unhappy.

    B: What's the _____ , he never listens.

i) A: I'm sure he won't want to go out with me. What's the point of asking him?

    B: Well, nothing _____ , nothing _____ .

🌐 39 Listen and check.

6 Look at the example and write similar sentences using *What's the point of …, if … .* Add two sentences of your own.

a) buy a piano / not going to learn to play it

    What's the point of buying a piano if you're not going to learn to play it?

b) have a well-paid job / never spend anything

    _____

    _____

c) go on holiday / always phoning the office

    _____

    _____

d) join a gym / never go

    _____

    _____

e) get a new mobile / nothing wrong with your old one

    _____

    _____

f) _____

    _____

    _____

g) _____

    _____

    _____

Pronunciation

1 🌐 40 Listen to these sentences and underline the most stressed word in each sentence.

a) Russia is far bigger than China.

b) The book is way better than the film.

2 Which do you think is the most stressed word in each sentence?

a) Computer games are way better than they used to be.

b) The film is nowhere near as good as the book.

c) Canada is only slightly bigger than the USA.

d) Soccer is nothing like as popular as baseball.

e) The bus is only a bit cheaper than the train.

f) Computers are infinitely more user-friendly these days.

🌐 41 Listen and check. Repeat the sentences.

Listening

1   🌐 42 You are going to listen to a radio interview with Hannah, who backpacked around Vietnam. As you listen, put the following topics into the order in which she talks about them.

a) The places she visited ☐

b) The impact of tourists ☐

c) The Vietnamese people ☐

d) Her first impressions of Vietnam ☐

e) How she travelled around the country ☐

2   Answer the questions. Listen again to check.

a) Hannah's first impressions of Vietnam were generally

  1 positive   2 negative   3 indifferent

b) Hannah was surprised that Saigon was so

  1 modern   2 busy   3 interesting

c) Tourists in Vietnam tend to

  1 stay in just on place   2 take different routes
  3 take the same route

d) Travelling around Vietnam is

  1 frustrating   2 easy   3 difficult

e) How does Hannah feel about visiting 'minority villages'?

  1 She thinks it is fine.
  2 She thinks we shouldn't do it.
  3 She thinks it is both a good and a bad thing.

f) Circle the words that describe the Vietnamese people according to Hannah.

  caring   happy   helpful   unhelpful

  indifferent   delicate   welcoming

  relaxed   friendly

3   Hannah says, 'I would suggest the 'leave only footprints' motto.' What does she mean by this?

_____

_____

4   Complete these expressions from the listening with the words in the box. What do the expressions mean? Listen again and check.

atmosphere   bustle   by   out   path   place

a) hustle and _____

b) a happening _____

c) a well-trodden _____

d) worth checking _____

e) soak up the _____

f) watch the world go _____

Presenter: Hannah, what were your first impressions of Vietnam?

Hannah: I was amazed from the moment I arrived in Saigon. The city is huge, jammed with traffic and people on the move everywhere. The backpacker area was really a happening place with lots of hustle and bustle. It's a very exciting city and there's so much to see and do in Saigon. And it's really quite modern, which I wasn't expecting.

Presenter: And you travelled around the country, didn't you?

Hannah: Yes, from south to north. It's a long narrow country, so the route you take is pretty well determined for you. It's a well-trodden path and you keep seeing the same faces all the time. The best way to get around is by bus. You can hop on and off along the way whenever and wherever you like – it's very well set up. For me the highlights were Hue, which if you're interested in the Vietnam War, then this is the place to get your fix. And I loved Hanoi, the capital, which is a beautiful city and much more unspoilt than Saigon – there are lots of amazing little markets that are definitely worth checking out. It's the perfect place to soak up the atmosphere and watch the world go by. From there we went to Sapa, in the very north, which has some great walks in the hills through lots of tiny 'minority' villages.

Presenter: Your experiences of 'minority' villages in Vietnam were mixed. Tell us a bit about this.

Hannah: Well, this whole issue is very delicate. As tourists we want to find the 'authentic' thing – remote, untouched, traditional villages. Yet the moment that tourists go to such places we affect them and disrupt the authenticity. It's a real dilemma though, as visiting these villages does generate money for the people who live there.

Presenter: So how can backpackers ensure that they don't have a negative impact on villagers?

Hannah: I would suggest the 'leave only footprints' motto and don't give money directly to locals as it does affect the local economy on a dramatic scale. It's important to support sustainable tourism, leaving the minimum possible impact on the society that you have infiltrated.

Presenter: And finally, if it's possible to generalise, what are the Vietnamese people like?

Hannah: I found them to be very easy-going and friendly. I think that the Buddhist religion encourages that. Lots of good karma. Most people along the way were very happy to help us and we felt very welcome at all times.

Writing

Writing an email recommending places to visit
Phrases for making recommendations

1 Think about and make a few notes about places in your country that you would recommend to a tourist.

2 Read Martina's email to Patrick opposite. What does she want to know?

3 Read Patrick's reply to Martina opposite. Which of the following does he recommend?

a) Spending some time in Kathmandu. ☐
b) Going to the Monkey Temple. ☐
c) Starting a trek from Kathmandu. ☐
d) Flying from Kathmandu to Pokara. ☐
e) Watching a sunset over the Himalays. ☐
f) Staying in local villages when trekking. ☐
g) Giving money to the local children. ☐
h) Visiting the jungle. ☐

4 Here are some useful phrases for recommending places to visit. Add the missing word. Then check in Patrick's email to Martina.

a) It's definitely _____ spending/visiting …
b) There's lots to _____ and do …
c) It's a great place _____ wander round / soak up the atmosphere / meet people …
d) The best way to _____ around is …
e) If you're _____ in …, then…
f) _____ you do, you must …
g) The best way to _____ there is …
h) Make _____ you …
i) Don't be _____ to …
j) If you _____ time, …
k) For a _____ of scene, you could …

5 A friend is planning to visit your country for the first time and has emailed you asking for some recommendations. You are going to write an email in reply. Plan your email as follows:
• use the notes you made in Exercise 1
• use the email in Exercise 3 as a model
• use some of the phrases in Exercise 4.

6 Write your email. You should write about 250 words.

Hi Patrick,

Just a quick email to let you know I'm thinking of going to Nepal for three weeks later in the year.

I know you've been there a couple of times and was just wondering if I could pick your brains about where you'd recommend and about things to see and do, and anything else you think might be useful. I definitely want to do some trekking and I'd like to see a few different places as well.

Thanks and hope you're well,

Martina x

Hi Martina,

It's great to hear from you and it's great that you are planning to visit Nepal. It's a truly amazing place.

Firstly, I'd say it's definitely worth spending a few days at least in Kathmandu, the capital. There's lots to see and do and it's a great place to wander round just soaking up the atmosphere. The best way to get around is on foot. There are a couple of places that are a rickshaw ride away – there's an ancient town called Bhaktapur and if you're interested in temples, there's an amazing one at Pashupatinath. And whatever you do, you must go to the Monkey Temple that overlooks Kathmandu. The views are just stunning.

As for trekking, it depends how long you want to trek for. Most of the treks start from a town called Pokara in the west of the country. There are several different treks of different lengths, so I'd suggest you get yourself to Pokara and see how much time you have and then decide. The best way to get there is by bus from Kathmandu – it's pretty scary though on the mountain roads.

And make sure you get up before dawn one morning and watch the sunrise over the Himalays. It's something you'll never forget.

You'll go through lots of small villages. Some have cafés and small guest houses, which are great places to stay, but try not to make too much impact as you trek through – don't be tempted to give the children money and things.

And if you have time, and for a change of scene, you could spend a few days in the jungle in Chitwan National Park – elephants, rhinos and, if you're lucky, tigers.

Anyway, let me know if you have any other questions. But I'm sure you'll work it all out when you get there.

Love,

Patrick

11 Words

Grammar

1 Look at the text below. Match the words in bold (*1–12*) to the words or phrases (*a–h*) they have substituted for. Some words and phrases may be used more than once.

Do you write text messages? I'm sure you (1) **do**. Everyone (2) **does** these days. But do you think (3) **they** affect the way you read and write? Many literacy experts think they (4) **can** – and (5) **do**, especially among adolescents. (6) **They** argue that text messages, and in particular the shorthand used to write (7) **them**, can damage young people's reading and writing skills. The disregard for conventional grammar and spelling shown in (8) **them** is seen as a threat. However, (9) **others** argue that reading and writing sms messages requires a sophisticated knowledge of the rules underlying the language. It is certainly true that since text messages became popular, young people have started writing much more than they ever (10) **did** (11) **before**. And writing has taken on a new importance in people's lives. It's now cool to (12) **do it**. And texting is especially cool.

a) affect the way we write
b) before sms messages were invented
c) literacy experts
d) text messages
e) texting
f) write(s) text messages
g) writing text messages
h) write
i) wrote

1	2	3	4	5	6	7	8	9	10	11	12
f											

2 Look at the conversation below. Make it as short as possible. Use substitution where necessary.

A: It's Tom's 30th birthday party tonight. Are you going ~~to the party~~? If ⌃so ~~you're going to the party~~, I can give you a lift.

B: Where is the party taking place?

A: The party's taking place at his brother's bar, I think.

B: Nobody told me anything about the party. Maybe I haven't been invited to go to the party. Are you going?

A: Yes, Tom invited me to the party last week when I saw Tom at the golf club. We were both at the golf club with our bosses. Our bosses play golf together every Thursday.

B: I didn't know your boss played with Tom's boss. How long have they been playing golf together every week?

A: They've been playing together for as long as I can remember. Anyway, going back to Tom's party, you should definitely come. I'm sure Tom will be disappointed if you don't come to his party. I'll see you at Tom's party.

🔘 43 Listen and compare your version with the recording.

Pronunciation

1 🔘 44 Listen to these short exchanges. Cross out any words you don't actually hear.

A: Are you ready to go out?
B: No, not yet, I'm just finishing this bit of work.
A: OK, we'll meet you there, then.
B: Yeah, I'll be there in about half an hour.
A: OK. We'll catch you later!

A: Did you see John last night?
B: No, was he supposed to be there then?
A: As far as I know, yes.
B: Hm. He must have got caught up at work or something.
A: I suppose so.

2 🔘 45 Listen again and repeat.

Vocabulary

1 **Match the words on the left with the words on the right to form compound nouns.**

a) always
b) conspicuous
c) credit
d) digital
e) face
f) lipstick

1 consumerism
2 crunch
3 down time
4 economy
5 connected
6 time

2 **Complete the sentences using the compound nouns from Exercise 1.**

a) Life has certainly become more stressful with the ___always connected___ lifestyle that most business people live these days.

b) In a _____ consumers spend on small luxury items rather than splurge on expensive indulgences.

c) The shop keepers are the first to suffer in a _____ , with shoppers cutting back on expenditure across the board.

d) Flash cars, furs coats, diamond-coated mobile phones are all hallmarks of the super rich and their _____ .

e) It's really important to make sure you fit in some quality _____ when you switch off your mobile, unplug your laptop and just relax.

f) At the end of a long day in front of my computer screen, I really appreciate simple, old-fashioned _____ with the people I love!

3 **Choose the correct prefix or suffix from the box to complete the definitions.**

ista	life	ography	right	speak	up

a) _right_ sizing: reducing the number of staff who work for a company

b) _____ skill : to improve your qualifications.

c) Phone_____ : photos taken on mobile phones

d) Net_____ : the language used by people communicating on the internet.

e) _____ casting : writing about day to day life on a blog or social network.

f) recession_____ : a person who dresses stylishly and sets trends without spending a lot of money.

4 **Replace the words in italics with the words and phrases below.**

favour	~~glean~~	going around the houses
hit the right note	put his point across	
rambling	tangents	sank in

a) Younger users tend to *pick up* information from visual sources much quicker than older users.
_____glean_____

b) Most teenagers *give preference to* texting over speaking. _____

c) When writing an essay, remember to answer the question and do not go off on unnecessary *explanations or descriptions that are irrelevant to the topic.* _____

d) The plot is interesting, but her style is marred by long, *endless and pointless* sentences that seem to go nowhere. _____

e) Stop *avoiding the issue* for goodness sake and get to the point! _____

f) I think he *explained himself* very succinctly.
_____

g) Well done! You really managed to *create the right effect* – encouraging without being too patronising. _____

h) He watched the expression on her face change as the meaning of his words *was* slowly *absorbed.*
_____

5 **Use the same word to complete both phrases in each pair.**

1 a) You're twisting my _____ .
  b) You're deliberately misconstruing my _____ .

2 a) My _____ is …
  b) You're missing the _____ .

3 a) I'm just _____ , …
  b) What I'm _____ is …

4 a) That's not _____ I'm saying.
  b) So _____ are you implying?

5 a) _____ is not what I meant.
  b) I didn't say _____ !

Reading

1 Read the article and choose the best title.

  a) How to Write a Cover Letter

  b) Top Five Cover Letter Blunders

  c) The Dos and Don'ts of applying for a job

2 Add the extracts (*a–e*) to the end of sections *1–5*.

  a) For example, mentioning that you are a qualified language teacher while applying for the post of civil engineer would not help your case.

  b) If you are applying to a company that greatly values teamwork, for instance, citing that you organised a community fund-raiser or played on a basketball team will probably be advantageous. But, when in doubt, leave it out.

  c) For example, I am very interested in this product development position, and I am confident in my ability to make a long-term contribution to your company.

  d) Indicating application for one position and mentioning a different position in the body of the letter.

  e) In general, using the first person voice is preferable.

🌐 **46 Listen and check.**

3 Find words in the article that mean:

  a) put something in danger _____

  b) wrong _____

  c) to make or change something especially for a particular person or purpose _____

  d) put across, communicate _____

  e) a promise or commitment _____

  f) is relevant _____

  g) making you feel confused or surprised _____

  h) a mistake made when typing _____

A cover letter is the letter (or, more usually, email message) you write to accompany a CV when you apply for a job. It is almost as important as your CV. It introduces you and helps create a first impression. You need to make sure that impression is a positive one. There are certain common errors that can jeopardise your hard work of writing a cover letter. From typing mishaps to erroneous employer information, all mistakes have a negative impact on the application process. Serious errors will land your application in the wastebasket. Be forewarned: carefully read your cover letter at least twice. The following list outlines some of the most common cover letter mistakes and, more importantly, suggests ways to correct them.

1 Unrelated Career Goals

Tailor your cover letter to the specific position applied for. Your letter should convey a genuine interest in the position and a long-term pledge to fulfilling its duties. ___

2 Unnecessary Career Information

Since cover letters are generally short, every word of every sentence should be directly related to your purpose for writing. Any other information weakens your application. ___

3 Irrelevant Personal Information

Do not include your age, weight, height, marital status, race, religion, or any other personal information unless you feel that it directly pertains to the position that you're seeking. For instance, height and weight may be important if you are applying to an athletic team. Similarly, you should list your personal interests and hobbies only if they are directly relevant to the type of job you are seeking. ___

4 Choice of Pronouns

Although some applicants might choose the third person ('he' or 'she') as a creative approach to presenting their qualifications, potential employers sometimes find this voice disconcerting. ___

5 Typos and editing errors

It is very easy to make mistakes in your letters, particularly when you are writing many in succession. But it is also very easy for a recruitment manager to reject out of hand any cover letter that contains errors, even those that seem minor at first glance. Here are a few common technical mistakes to watch out for when proof reading your letter:

• Misspelling the recruitment manager's name or title in the address, in the greeting, or on the envelope.

• Forgetting to change the name of the organisation you're applying to each time it appears in your application, especially in the body of the letter.

• ___

Writing

Writing a cover letter
Cover letter conventions
Spelling

1 Look at this checklist of things to remember when writing an email to accompany a job application. Put a tick (✓) for the Dos and a cross (✗) for the Don'ts.

a) forget to use paragraphs to separate the three sections of your letter

b) use contracted forms or abbreviations

c) be as polite as you would if you were meeting the person for the first time

d) include irrelevant information

e) use a spell check and proof read your letter carefully

f) use the subject line to explain why you are writing

g) duplicate information included in your CV

h) attach a CV in a separate document

i) leave the recipient's name out and forget to sign off as in a normal letter

j) be too chatty or informal as you would in an email to a friend

k) explain which post you are applying for

l) keep it brief and to the point

2 Read this email cover letter and answer the questions.

a) What position is the person applying for?

b) What points on the checklist has he forgotten?

From: Robbie
To: **staffing@dunroe.co.uk**
Subject: re post of freelance translator
Attachment: Robbie's CV

I'm writing to aply for the post of freelance translator advertised in the Guardian on February 27th. I graduated in English and Europaen Studies at the University of Naples in 1996. After graduating I worked for six months as a traine in a local trade journal but decided that I didn't like the job and left to study for my translator exams. I passed these in June 1997 and then wnet on to work for a series of small translation agencies in my home town.

I am curently looking for a more permenent position which will allow me to improve my skils and develop as a translator. I think your company will benefit form my expereince and my abilities. I am available for interveiw any time next week.

That's all for now,

Robbie

3 Find and correct ten typos or spelling mistakes in the email.

_____   _____

_____   _____

_____   _____

_____   _____

_____   _____

4 Underline the phrases Robbie uses to explain

a) why he's writing

b) why he is interested in the post

c) what he has to offer

d) when he can attend an interview

5 You are going to apply for the same job as Robbie. Write a cover letter to accompany your CV. Invent any information you need to. Use the format below to help you. You should write approximately 250 words.

Dear Mr/Ms Last Name, (*If you don't know their name:* Dear sir or madam,)

First paragraph

Why you are writing

Remember to make a clear reference to the post you are applying for.

Notes _____

_____

_____

Middle paragraphs

1 *Why you are interested*

Remember to include a short description of your current work position.

Notes _____

_____

_____

2 *What you have to offer*

Convince the readers that you are a suitable candidate and that they should call you for interview. Make connections between your abilities and the job requirements in the advert.

Notes _____

_____

_____

Final paragraph

Remember to let the readers know when you are available for interview and how best to get in touch with you. Include a phone number and times when you can be reached on it.

Notes _____

_____

_____

Yours sincerely, (*or* Yours faithfully *if you don't know the person's name*)

Your name

12 Conscience

Grammar

1 Match sentences *a–g* to responses *1–7*.

a) I really am fed up with always putting my hand in my pocket.
b) We're running a bit late.
c) She is really tired and needs a break.
d) My car keeps breaking down.
e) His exam results are getting worse.
f) John really hasn't got the experience to run the project.
g) I don't agree with giving money to charities.

1 I wish I could spend more time with him to help him with his studies.
2 I'd rather we recruited someone with more of a background in this area.
3 I think it's time we made a move.
4 It's high time he learnt to pay his own way.
5 If only I had the money to buy a new one.
6 I'd rather people volunteered some of their time.
7 It's time she had a holiday.

a	b	c	d	e	f	g
4						

2 Correct the mistakes in these sentences.

a) I'm really unfit. I think it's time I ~~join~~ *joined* a gym.

b) She'd rather spent the weekend in a quiet country village than in a busy city.

c) I wish I don't have to work today. I'm feeling really tired.

d) If only there wouldn't be so much bureaucracy involved in charity work.

e) She wishes she can come with us on holiday but her work commitments are going to keep her at home.

f) I'd rather you not do that. It might be dangerous.

g) It really is high time the government would do something more concrete to help the homeless.

h) He said he'd rather I might give the presentation, as I've done it before and I know what's needed.

3 Complete the second sentence so that it means the same as the first.

a) I really think the local authorities should do something about the traffic.

It's high time *the local authorities did something about the traffic.*

b) Please don't smoke in my car.

I'd rather _____
_____

c) I think someone needs to teach him a few manners. He's very rude.

It's high time _____
_____

d) I really think he should stop wasting time and settle down to a good job.

It's about time _____
_____

e) I'd prefer you to stay at home and look after the children so that I can go shopping.

I'd rather _____
_____
_____

Pronunciation

1 🔊 47 Listen to four short exchanges. Mark the main stress in each of the answers.

So, I hear you did a parachute jump for charity.

a) No, I did a bungee jump.
b) No, that was my sister, not me.
c) No, I did it for fun.
d) No, but I'm thinking of doing one.

Why does the stress fall on these words?

2 Look at the four responses below. Where does the main stress fall in each one?

So, you were collecting money for Oxfam.

a) No, for Comic Relief, actually.
b) No, we were collecting old clothes.
c) No, I was ill that day, but my brother went.
d) Erm, no, for our school, actually.

🔊 48 Listen and check.

Vocabulary

1 Decide which word is the odd one out in each list (a–c) and then choose the correct explanation (1–3) for your answers.

a) homeless person   street performer   wino
b) beggars   buskers   squeegee merchants
c) bag lady   down-and-out   street person

1 It's more formal than the other two.
2 It's informal, the other two are formal.
3 They don't do anything to earn the money they're given.

2 Underline the correct verb.

a) The families were finally **reunited** / secured last night after three harrowing days of uncertainty.

b) The course seeks to help trainees **represent** / **secure** employment in the airline industry.

c) It's high time the government started **addressing** / **pursuing** the issue of teenage drinking, before we become a nation of alcoholics!

d) More and more girls are choosing to **pursue** / **represent** a career in previously male-dominated fields such as engineering.

e) It is an immense honour to be called to **boost** / **represent** my country in the Olympics.

f) Winning that prize in the dance competition has really helped to **address** / **boost** her self-esteem. She's much happier now.

3 Complete the sentences with the words in the box.

| my | an | on | guilty | her | a̶ |
| in | c̶l̶e̶a̶r̶ | easy | all | ease | a |

a) I know I didn't have anything to do with it. I've got ___a___ ___clear___ conscience.

b) I can't see how she'll ever forget the incident. It'll be _____ _____ conscience forever.

c) _____ _____ conscience, can you really say that when you see people begging for money on the street, you don't feel bad?

d) Thanks for popping in and checking on my grandmother. It helps _____ _____ conscience. I'm worried about leaving her on her own.

e) Don't worry. Our company will look after all the arrangements so that you can enjoy the day with _____ _____ conscience.

f) She's suffering from _____ _____ conscience. She knows it was her fault and feels terrible.

4 Write the words in the correct order to make apologies. Add punctuation.

a) sorry   really   I'm   again   happen   won't   It
I'm really sorry. It won't happen again.

b) apology   you   think   an   I   owe   I
_____

c) seat   idea   your   Sorry   was   I   no   had   this
_____

d) mind   my   sorry   slipped   I'm   totally   it
_____

e) sorry   am   really   terribly   I   idea   I   no   had
_____

f) bad   weather   We   all   trains   cancelled   have been   to   inform   regret   you   due   to   that
_____
_____

5 Match the apologies in Exercise 4 to the responses 1–6 below.

1 [f] Again! They're forever doing this to me!
2 [   ] It better hadn't! We can't afford another mistake like that!
3 [   ] It's OK. You can stay there. It doesn't really matter.
4 [   ] You most certainly do!
5 [   ] That's OK. You weren't to know.
6 [   ] No worries, it wasn't important.

🌐 49 Listen and check.

Listening

1   ● 50 Cover the script and listen to a radio interview with a volunteer worker for a charity called Comic Relief. Answer these questions.

   a)   When was the charity founded? _____

   b)   Why was it founded? _____
        _____
        _____

   c)   Why is it called Comic Relief? _____
        _____

   d)   What's the name of the main event organised by this charity? _____

   e)   What sort of activities do the fund-raisers get involved in?_____
        _____

2   **Which of these topics are *not* discussed?**

   a)   the people who founded the charity

   b)   the main difference between Comic Relief and other charity organisations

   c)   the amount of money raised

   d)   the projects funded by the charity

   e)   the main fund-raising events

   f)   the celebrities who support the cause

   Listen to the interview again to check.

3   **Complete the extracts below with the words in the box.**

   ┌─────────────────────────────────────┐
   │ catchy   devastating   good   │
   │ organised   refugee   role   silly │
   └─────────────────────────────────────┘

   a)   At the time there was a _____ famine in Sudan and Ethiopia.

   b)   The charity was launched from a _____ camp in Sudan …

   c)   Yes, the appeal of doing something silly in a _____ cause is very powerful.

   d)   … basically, we were looking around for a _____ symbol …

   e)   … people love the sponsored _____ -reversal events – bosses get sponsored to be a secretary for the day …

   f)   … then there are the _____ events, like the Red Nose Fun Run …

   g)   … with thousands of runners jogging through the City of London in various _____ costumes.

Interviewer:	Today, in the studio, we're pleased to welcome Janet Whittall, our local Comic Relief organiser. Hello, Janet. Thanks for being with us here today.
Janet:	It's a pleasure.
Interviewer:	So, could you tell us a little bit of the history behind Comic Relief? When did it first start up?
Janet:	Erm, yeah, well, it first started up in 1985. At the time there was a devastating famine in Sudan and Ethiopia. The charity was launched from a refugee camp in Sudan on Christmas Day to raise funds for the victims of the famine. But they also wanted to look at the more widespread needs of the poor in that region, and indeed of poor and disadvantaged people all over the world.
Interviewer:	But why Comic Relief? What's the story behind the name?
Janet:	Well, basically it's called Comic Relief because it was first set up by comedians and because it uses comedy and laughter to get its message across. That's what makes it unique.
Interviewer:	And it's been incredibly successful.
Janet:	Yes, the appeal of doing something silly in a good cause is very powerful. Did you know that in 2009 more than 80 million pounds were raised on Red Nose Day?
Interviewer:	How did the idea for Red Nose Day come about?
Janet:	Well, basically, we were looking around for a catchy symbol, something that would be cheap and easy for everyone to use. And the traditional red nose worn by circus clowns really fits the bill – on Red Nose Day you can see them everywhere, not only on people's faces. You see them stuck on the front of cars, buses and even underground trains.
Interviewer:	But there's more to Red Nose Day than wearing red noses.
Janet:	Yes, there's all kinds of sponsored silliness going on … people love the sponsored role-reversal events – bosses get sponsored to be a secretary for the day, or pupils sponsor their teachers to wear a school uniform – and then there are the organised events, like the Red Nose Fun Run, with thousands of runners jogging through the city of London in various silly costumes.
Interviewer:	So, what will you be doing on Red Nose Day this year?
Janet:	We're holding a huge Red Dinner Party in the centre of town. Everyone has to dress in red, bring along some red food and of course pay a generous bill which will all go to Comic Relief … What about you?
Interviewer:	The staff here at the radio station have sponsored me to shave my head and have a red dragon painted on it.

Writing

Writing a promotional flyer
Text organisation
Style and register

1 Read this flyer advertising a charity fund-raising event. The paragraphs (*a–d*) are not in the correct order. Reorder them so that they match the paragraph headings.

Coming soon to an office, school, shop or street near you ....

**ALL CHANGE!!!
The charity role
reversal game**

1 SO, WHAT'S IT ALL ABOUT?
a) OK! Here's what you have to do. On Friday 15 June, go to work, or to school, or shopping or whatever you normally do, dressed as normal, BUT on your head you must wear the most outrageous, unbelieveable headgear you can possibly find! Are you a policeman but would really love to be a chef? Are you a secretary with secret yearnings to be a Hollywood princess? Or a baker who wants to wear the world's largest wig? Now's your chance! Be creative!

2 WHEN DID IT GET GOING?
b) Great! We want 100, 000 or more people like you to bring a smile to the face of local children. To find out more contact us on our website or phone 502 389 711. And remember, for the sake of children ...

3 WANT TO TAKE PART?
c) *All Change!* is a fantastic, fun-filled, fancy dress festival that will help us to raise money for children in need.

4 STILL WANT TO TAKE PART?
d) The first *All change!* role reversal extravaganza took place in 2005 in aid of a local children's charity. Every year since then nearly 100,000 men, women and children have donned the weirdest and wonderfullest headgear possible to raise money for a growing number of children's charities. This year we are helping a record number of good causes, all aimed to help children in need.

**IT'S TIME FOR A CHANGE
On Friday 15 June
It's ALL CHANGE DAY!!**

2 Match the paragraphs (*a–d*) on the flyer to the following summaries.

1 a short description of the history behind the event and the cause it's raising money for

2 details of what exactly the event involves

3 details about how to get involved

4 an introduction to the event

3 Which of the following descriptions best describes the style of the flyer?

a) It is serious and informative, appealing to the reader's sense of fair play and social conscience by including facts and figures about the causes the charity supports.

b) It is fun and informative. It seems to be speaking directly to the reader. It uses questions, exclamations and adjectives very much as we would in speech.

c) It is fun and appeals to the reader's sense of humour, using jokes and rhymes to make its point. It does not, however, include any factual information about the charity or the event.

Underline any specific language in the flyer that supports your answer.

4 Choose the option which is most likely to appear on the *All Change!* website.

1 a) Come and join the fun!
   b) We invite you to come and join us in our campaign.

2 a) Fancy seeing your boss in a Roman centurian's helmet?
   b) Maybe you can persuade your boss to wear a Roman centurian's helmet for the day?

3 a) We're sure everyone who takes part will have plenty of fun.
   b) There's fun and laughs for all the family!

4 a) And you will go away knowing that you have helped a good cause.
   b) It's a great chance to help a great cause!

5 You are going to write a flyer for a similar fund-raising event. Follow the steps below.

• Decide on the kind of event you are going to advertise. It should be fun and appeal to as many people as possible. It might be a fun run, a sponsored dance, a costume idea (such as the red nose or the headgear), etc.

• Decide what charity you are raising money for.

• Think of a catchy slogan or name for your event.

• Draw up a flyer using headings, sub-headings and short, clear paragraphs. Remember to use questions, exclamations and adjectives as in the model above.

You should write approximately 250 words.

Story: *The Terror of Blue John Gap*

By Sir Arthur Conan Doyle

The following narrative was found among the papers of Dr. James Hardcastle, who died of phthisis* on February 4th, 1908, at 36, Upper Coventry Flats, South Kensington. Those who knew him best, while refusing to express an opinion upon this particular statement, are unanimous in asserting that he was a man of a sober and scientific turn of mind, absolutely devoid of imagination, and most unlikely to invent any abnormal series of events. The paper was contained in an envelope, which was docketed, 'A Short Account of the Circumstances which occurred near Miss Allerton's Farm in North-West Derbyshire in the Spring of Last Year.' The envelope was sealed, and on the other side was written in pencil –

DEAR SEATON, –

'It may interest, and perhaps pain you, to know that the incredulity with which you met my story has prevented me from ever opening my mouth upon the subject again. I leave this record after my death, and perhaps strangers may be found to have more confidence in me than my friend.'

Inquiry has failed to elicit who this Seaton may have been. I may add that the visit of the deceased to Allerton's Farm, and the general nature of the alarm there, apart from his particular explanation, have been absolutely established. With this foreword I append his account exactly as he left it. It is in the form of a diary, some entries in which have been expanded, while a few have been erased.

———

April 17. Already I feel the benefit of this wonderful upland air. The farm of the Allertons lies fourteen hundred and twenty feet above sea-level, so it may well be a bracing climate. Beyond the usual morning cough I have very little discomfort, and, what with the fresh milk and the home-grown mutton, I have every chance of putting on weight. I think Saunderson will be pleased.

The two Miss Allertons are charmingly quaint and kind, two dear little hard-working old maids, who are ready to lavish all the heart which might have gone out to husband and to children upon an invalid stranger. Truly, the old maid is a most useful person, one of the reserve forces of the community. They talk of the superfluous woman, but what would the poor superfluous man do without her kindly presence? By the way, in their simplicity they very quickly let out the reason why Saunderson recommended their farm. The Professor rose from the ranks himself, and I believe that in his youth he was not above scaring crows in these very fields.

It is a most lonely spot, and the walks are picturesque in the extreme. The farm consists of grazing land lying at the bottom of an irregular valley. On each side are the fantastic limestone hills, formed of rock so soft that you can break it away with your hands. All this country is hollow. Could you strike it with some gigantic hammer it would boom like a drum, or possibly cave in altogether and expose some huge subterranean sea. A great sea there must surely be, for on all sides the streams run into the mountain itself, never to reappear. There are gaps everywhere amid the rocks, and when you pass through them you find yourself in great caverns, which wind down into the bowels of the earth. I have a small bicycle lamp, and it is a perpetual joy to me to carry it into these weird solitudes, and to see the wonderful silver and black effect when I throw its light upon the stalactites which drape the lofty roofs. Shut off the lamp, and you are in the blackest darkness. Turn it on, and it is a scene from the Arabian Nights.

But there is one of these strange openings in the earth which has a special interest, for it is the handiwork, not of nature, but of man. I had

———

* tuberculosis

never heard of Blue John when I came to these parts. It is the name given to a peculiar mineral of a beautiful purple shade, which is only found at one or two places in the world. It is so rare that an ordinary vase of Blue John would be valued at a great price. The Romans, with that extraordinary instinct of theirs, discovered that it was to be found in this valley, and sank a horizontal shaft deep into the mountain side. The opening of their mine has been called Blue John Gap, a clean-cut arch in the rock, the mouth all overgrown with bushes. It is a goodly passage which the Roman miners have cut, and it intersects some of the great water-worn caves, so that if you enter Blue John Gap you would do well to mark your steps and to have a good store of candles, or you may never make your way back to the daylight again. I have not yet gone deeply into it, but this very day I stood at the mouth of the arched tunnel, and peering down into the black recesses beyond, I vowed that when my health returned I would devote some holiday to exploring those mysterious depths and finding out for myself how far the Romans had penetrated into the Derbyshire hills.

Strange how superstitious these countrymen are! I should have thought better of young Armitage, for he is a man of some education and character, and a very fine fellow for his station in life. I was standing at the Blue John Gap when he came across the field to me.

'Well, doctor,' said he, 'you're not afraid, anyhow.'

'Afraid!' I answered. 'Afraid of what?'

'Of it,' said he, with a jerk of his thumb towards the black vault, 'of the Terror that lives in the Blue John Cave.'

How absurdly easy it is for a legend to arise in a lonely countryside! I examined him as to the reasons for his weird belief. It seems that from time to time sheep have been missing from the fields, carried bodily away, according to Armitage. That they could have wandered away of their own accord and disappeared among the mountains was an explanation to which he would not listen. On one occasion a pool of blood had been found, and some tufts of wool. That also, I pointed out, could be explained in a perfectly natural way. Further,

the nights upon which sheep disappeared were invariably very dark, cloudy nights with no moon. This I met with the obvious retort that those were the nights which a commonplace sheep-stealer would naturally choose for his work. On one occasion a gap had been made in a wall, and some of the stones scattered for a considerable distance. Human agency again, in my opinion. Finally, Armitage clinched all his arguments by telling me that he had actually heard the Creature – indeed, that anyone could hear it who remained long enough at the Gap. It was a distant roaring of an immense volume. I could not but smile at this, knowing, as I do, the strange reverberations which come out of an underground water system running amid the chasms of a limestone formation. My incredulity annoyed Armitage so that he turned and left me with some abruptness.

And now comes the queer point about the whole business. I was still standing near the mouth of the cave turning over in my mind the various statements of Armitage, and reflecting how readily they could be explained away, when suddenly, from the depth of the tunnel beside me, there issued a most extraordinary sound. How shall I describe it? First of all, it seemed to be a great distance away, far down in the bowels of the earth. Secondly, in spite of this suggestion of distance, it was very loud. Lastly, it was not a boom, nor a crash, such as one would associate with falling water or tumbling rock, but it was a high whine, tremulous and vibrating, almost like the whinnying of a horse. It was certainly a most remarkable experience, and one which for a moment, I must admit, gave a new significance to Armitage's words. I waited by the Blue John Gap for half an hour or more, but there was no return of the sound, so at last I wandered back to the farmhouse, rather mystified by what had occurred. Decidedly I shall explore that cavern when my strength is restored. Of course, Armitage's explanation is too absurd for discussion, and yet that sound was certainly very strange. It still rings in my ears as I write.

———

April 20. In the last three days I have made several expeditions to the Blue John Gap, and have even penetrated some short distance, but my bicycle lantern is so small and weak that I dare not trust myself very far. I shall do the thing more systematically. I have heard no sound at all, and could almost believe that I had been the victim of some hallucination suggested, perhaps, by Armitage's conversation. Of course, the whole idea is absurd, and yet I must confess that those bushes at the entrance of the cave do present an appearance as if some heavy creature had forced its way through them. I begin to be keenly interested. I have said nothing to the Miss Allertons, for they are quite superstitious enough already, but I have bought some candles, and mean to investigate for myself.

I observed this morning that among the numerous tufts of sheep's wool which lay among the bushes near the cavern there was one which was smeared with blood. Of course, my reason tells me that if sheep wander into such rocky places they are likely to injure themselves, and yet somehow that splash of crimson gave me a sudden shock, and for a moment I found myself shrinking back in horror from the old Roman arch. A fetid breath seemed to ooze from the black depths into which I peered. Could it indeed be possible that some nameless thing, some dreadful presence, was lurking down yonder? I should have been incapable of such feelings in the days of my strength, but one grows more nervous and fanciful when one's health is shaken.

For the moment I weakened in my resolution, and was ready to leave the secret of the old mine, if one exists, for ever unsolved. But tonight my interest has returned and my nerves grown more steady. Tomorrow I trust that I shall have gone more deeply into this matter.

————

April 22. Let me try and set down as accurately as I can my extraordinary experience of yesterday. I started in the afternoon, and made my way to the Blue John Gap. I confess that my misgivings returned as I gazed into its depths, and I wished that I had brought a companion to share my exploration. Finally, with a return of resolution, I lit my candle, pushed my way through the briars, and descended into the rocky shaft.

It went down at an acute angle for some fifty feet, the floor being covered with broken stone. Thence there extended a long, straight passage cut in the solid rock. I am no geologist, but the lining of this corridor was certainly of some harder material than limestone, for there were points where I could actually see the tool-marks which the old miners had left in their excavation, as fresh as if they had been done yesterday. Down this strange, old-world corridor I stumbled, my feeble flame throwing a dim circle of light around me, which made the shadows beyond the more threatening and obscure. Finally, I came to a spot where the Roman tunnel opened into a water-worn cavern – a huge hall, hung with long white icicles of lime deposit. From this central chamber I could dimly perceive that a number of passages worn by the subterranean streams wound away into the depths of the earth. I was standing there wondering whether I had better return, or whether I dare venture farther into this dangerous labyrinth, when my eyes fell upon something at my feet which strongly arrested my attention.

The greater part of the floor of the cavern was covered with boulders of rock or with hard incrustations of lime, but at this particular point there had been a drip from the distant roof, which had left a patch of soft mud. In the very centre of this there was a huge mark – an ill-defined blotch, deep, broad and irregular, as if a great boulder had fallen upon it. No loose stone lay near, however, nor was there anything to account for the impression. It was far too large to be caused by any possible animal, and besides, there was only the one, and the patch of mud was of such a size that no reasonable stride could have covered it. As I rose from the examination of that singular mark and then looked round into the black shadows which hemmed me in, I must confess that I felt for a moment a most unpleasant sinking of my heart, and that, do what I could, the candle trembled in my outstretched hand.

I soon recovered my nerve, however, when I reflected how absurd it was to associate so huge and shapeless a mark with the track of any known animal. Even an elephant could not have produced it. I determined, therefore, that I would not be scared by vague and senseless fears from carrying out my exploration. Before proceeding, I took good note of a curious rock formation in the wall by which I could recognize the entrance of the Roman tunnel. The precaution was very

   The Terror of Blue John Gap

necessary, for the great cave, so far as I could see it, was intersected by passages. Having made sure of my position, and reassured myself by examining my spare candles and my matches, I advanced slowly over the rocky and uneven surface of the cavern.

And now I come to the point where I met with such sudden and desperate disaster. A stream, some twenty feet broad, ran across my path, and I walked for some little distance along the bank to find a spot where I could cross dry-shod. Finally, I came to a place where a single flat boulder lay near the centre, which I could reach in a stride. As it chanced, however, the rock had been cut away and made top-heavy by the rush of the stream, so that it tilted over as I landed on it and shot me into the ice-cold water. My candle went out, and I found myself floundering about in utter and absolute darkness.

I staggered to my feet again, more amused than alarmed by my adventure. The candle had fallen from my hand, and was lost in the stream, but I had two others in my pocket, so that it was of no importance. I got one of them ready, and drew out my box of matches to light it. Only then did I realize my position. The box had been soaked in my fall into the river. It was impossible to strike the matches.

A cold hand seemed to close round my heart as I realized my position. The darkness was opaque and horrible. It was so utter, one put one's hand up to one's face as if to press off something solid. I stood still, and by an effort I steadied myself. I tried to reconstruct in my mind a map of the floor of the cavern as I had last seen it. Alas! The bearings which had impressed themselves upon my mind were high on the wall, and not to be found by touch. Still, I remembered in a general way how the sides were situated, and I hoped that by groping my way along them I should at last come to the opening of the Roman tunnel. Moving very slowly, and continually striking against the rocks, I set out on this desperate quest. But I very soon realized how impossible it was. In that black, velvety darkness one lost all one's bearings in an instant. Before I had made a dozen paces, I was utterly bewildered as to my whereabouts. The rippling of the stream, which was the one sound audible, showed me where it lay, but the moment that I left its bank I was utterly lost. The idea of finding my way back in absolute darkness through that limestone labyrinth was clearly an impossible one.

I sat down upon a boulder and reflected upon my unfortunate plight. I had not told anyone that I proposed to come to the Blue John mine, and it was unlikely that a search party would come after me. Therefore I must trust to my own resources to get clear of the danger. There was only one hope, and that was that the matches might dry. When I fell into the river, only half of me had got thoroughly wet. My left shoulder had remained above the water. I took the box of matches, therefore, and put it into my left armpit. The moist air of the cavern might possibly be counteracted by the heat of my body, but even so, I knew that I could not hope to get a light for many hours. Meanwhile there was nothing for it but to wait.

By good luck I had slipped several biscuits into my pocket before I left the farm-house. These I now devoured, and washed them down with a draught from that wretched stream which had been the cause of all my misfortunes. Then I felt about for a comfortable seat among the rocks, and, having discovered a place where I could get a support for my back, I stretched out my legs and settled myself down to wait. I was wretchedly damp and cold, but I tried to cheer myself with the reflection that modern science prescribed open windows and walks in all weather for my disease. Gradually, lulled by the monotonous gurgle of the stream, and by the absolute darkness, I sank into an uneasy slumber.

How long this lasted I cannot say. It may have been for an hour, it may have been for several. Suddenly I sat up on my rock couch, with every nerve thrilling and every sense acutely on the alert. Beyond all doubt I had heard a sound – some sound very distinct from the gurgling of the waters. It had passed, but the reverberation of it still lingered in my ear. Was it a search party? They would most certainly have shouted, and vague as this sound was which had wakened me, it was very distinct from the human voice. I sat palpitating and hardly daring to breathe. There it was again! And again! Now it had become continuous. It was a tread – yes, surely it was the tread of some living creature. But what a tread it was! It gave one the impression of enormous weight carried upon sponge-like feet, which gave forth a muffled but ear-filling sound. The darkness was as complete as ever, but the tread was regular and decisive. And it was coming beyond all question in my direction.

My skin grew cold, and my hair stood on end as I listened to that steady and ponderous footfall. There was some creature there, and surely by the speed of its advance, it was one which could see in the dark. I crouched low on my rock and tried to blend myself into it. The steps grew nearer still, then stopped, and presently I was aware of a loud lapping and gurgling. The creature was drinking at the stream. Then again there was silence, broken by a succession of long sniffs and snorts of tremendous volume and energy. Had it caught the scent of me? My own nostrils were filled by a low fetid odour, mephitic and abominable. Then I heard the steps again. They were on my side of the stream now. The stones rattled within a few yards of where I lay. Hardly daring to breathe, I crouched upon my rock. Then the steps drew away. I heard the splash as it returned across the river, and the sound died away into the distance in the direction from which it had come.

For a long time I lay upon the rock, too much horrified to move. I thought of the sound which I had heard coming from the depths of the cave, of Armitage's fears, of the strange impression in the mud, and now came this final and absolute proof that there was indeed some inconceivable monster, something utterly unearthly and dreadful, which lurked in the hollow of the mountain. Of its nature or form I could frame no conception, save that it was both light-footed and gigantic. The combat between my reason, which told me that such things could not be, and my senses, which told me that they were, raged within me as I lay. Finally, I was almost ready to persuade myself that this experience had been part of some evil dream, and that my abnormal condition might have conjured up an hallucination. But there remained one final experience which removed the last possibility of doubt from my mind.

I had taken my matches from my armpit and felt them. They seemed perfectly hard and dry. Stooping down into a crevice of the rocks, I tried one of them. To my delight it took fire at once. I lit the candle, and, with a terrified backward glance into the obscure depths of the cavern, I hurried in the direction of the Roman passage. As I did so I passed the patch of mud on which I had seen the huge imprint. Now I stood astonished before it, for there were three similar imprints upon its surface, enormous in size,

irregular in outline, of a depth which indicated the ponderous weight which had left them. Then a great terror surged over me. Stooping and shading my candle with my hand, I ran in a frenzy of fear to the rocky archway, hastened up it, and never stopped until, with weary feet and panting lungs, I rushed up the final slope of stones, broke through the tangle of briars, and flung myself exhausted upon the soft grass under the peaceful light of the stars. It was three in the morning when I reached the farm-house, and today I am all unstrung and quivering after my terrific adventure. As yet I have told no one. I must move warily in the matter. What would the poor lonely women, or the uneducated yokels here think of it if I were to tell them my experience? Let me go to someone who can understand and advise.

————

April 25. I was laid up in bed for two days after my incredible adventure in the cavern. I use the adjective with a very definite meaning, for I have had an experience since which has shocked me almost as much as the other. I have said that I was looking round for someone who could advise me. There is a Dr. Mark Johnson who practises some few miles away, to whom I had a note of recommendation from Professor Saunderson. To him I drove, when I was strong enough to get about, and I recounted to him my whole strange experience. He listened intently, and then carefully examined me, paying special attention to my reflexes and to the pupils of my eyes. When he had finished, he refused to discuss my adventure, saying that it was entirely beyond him, but he gave me the card of a Mr. Picton at Castleton, with the advice that I should instantly go to him and tell him the story exactly as I had done to himself. He was, according to my adviser, the very man who was pre-eminently suited to help me. I went on to the station, therefore, and made my way to the little town, which is some ten miles away. Mr. Picton appeared to be a man of importance, as his brass plate was displayed upon the door of a considerable building on the outskirts of the town. I was about to ring his bell, when some misgiving came into my mind, and, crossing to a neighbouring shop, I asked the man behind the counter if he could tell me anything of Mr. Picton. 'Why,' said he, 'he is the best mad doctor in Derbyshire, and yonder is his asylum.'

You can imagine that it was not long before I had shaken the dust of Castleton from my feet and returned to the farm, cursing all unimaginative pedants who cannot conceive that there may be things in creation which have never yet chanced to come across their mole's vision. After all, now that I am cooler, I can afford to admit that I have been no more sympathetic to Armitage than Dr. Johnson has been to me.

———

April 27. When I was a student I had the reputation of being a man of courage and enterprise. I remember that when there was a ghost-hunt at Coltbridge it was I who sat up in the haunted house. Is it advancing years (after all, I am only thirty-five), or is it this physical malady which has caused degeneration? Certainly my heart quails when I think of that horrible cavern in the hill, and the certainty that it has some monstrous occupant. What shall I do? There is not an hour in the day that I do not debate the question. If I say nothing, then the mystery remains unsolved. If I do say anything, then I have the alternative of mad alarm over the whole countryside, or of absolute incredulity which may end in consigning me to an asylum. On the whole, I think that my best course is to wait, and to prepare for some expedition which shall be more deliberate and better thought out than the last. As a first step I have been to Castleton and obtained a few essentials – a large acetylene lantern for one thing, and a good double-barrelled sporting rifle for another. The latter I have hired, but I have bought a dozen heavy game cartridges, which would bring down a rhinoceros. Now I am ready for my troglodyte friend. Give me better health and a little spate of energy, and I shall try conclusions with him yet. But who and what is he? Ah! there is the question which stands between me and my sleep. How many theories do I form, only to discard each in turn! It is all so utterly unthinkable. And yet the cry, the footmark, the tread in the cavern – no reasoning can get past these. I think of the old-world legends of dragons and of other monsters. Were they, perhaps, not such fairy tales as we have thought? Can it be that there is some fact which underlies them, and am I, of all mortals, the one who is chosen to expose it?

———

May 3. For several days I have been laid up by the vagaries of an English spring, and during those days there have been developments, the true and sinister meaning of which no one can appreciate save myself. I may say that we have had cloudy and moonless nights of late, which according to my information were the seasons upon which sheep disappeared. Well, sheep have disappeared. Two of Miss Allerton's, one of old Pearson's of the Cat Walk, and one of Mrs. Moulton's. Four in all during three nights. No trace is left of them at all, and the countryside is buzzing with rumours of gipsies and of sheep-stealers.

But there is something more serious than that. Young Armitage has disappeared also. He left his moorland cottage early on Wednesday night and has never been heard of since. He was an unattached man, so there is less sensation than would otherwise be the case. The popular explanation is that he owes money, and has found a situation in some other part of the country, whence he will presently write for his belongings. But I have grave misgivings. Is it not much more likely that the recent tragedy of those sheep has caused him to take some steps which may have ended in his own destruction? He may, for example, have lain in wait for the creature and been carried off by it into the recesses of the mountains. What an inconceivable fate for a civilized Englishman of the twentieth century! And yet I feel that it is possible and even probable. But in that case, how far am I answerable both for his death and for any other mishap which may occur? Surely with the knowledge I already possess it must be my duty to see that something is done, or if necessary to do it myself. It must be the latter, for this morning I went down to the local police-station and told my story. The inspector entered it all in a large book and bowed me out with commendable gravity, but I heard a burst of laughter before I had got down his garden path. No doubt he was recounting my adventure to his family.

———

June 10. I am writing this, propped up in bed, six weeks after my last entry in this journal. I have gone through a terrible shock both to mind and body, arising from such an experience as has seldom befallen a human being before. But I have attained my end. The danger from the Terror which dwells in the Blue John Gap has passed never to return. Thus much at least I, a broken invalid, have done for the common good. Let me now recount what occurred as clearly as I may.

The night of Friday, May 3rd, was dark and cloudy – the very night for the monster to walk. About eleven o'clock I went from the farm-house with my lantern and my rifle, having first left a note upon the table of my bedroom in which I said that, if I were missing, search should be made for me in the direction of the Gap. I made my way to the mouth of the Roman shaft, and, having perched myself among the rocks close to the opening, I shut off my lantern and waited patiently with my loaded rifle ready to my hand.

It was a melancholy vigil. All down the winding valley I could see the scattered lights of the farm-houses, and the church clock of Chapel-le-Dale tolling the hours came faintly to my ears. These tokens of my fellow-men served only to make my own position seem the more lonely, and to call for a greater effort to overcome the terror which tempted me continually to get back to the farm, and abandon for ever this dangerous quest. And yet there lies deep in every man a rooted self-respect which makes it hard for him to turn back from that which he has once undertaken. This feeling of personal pride was my salvation now, and it was that alone which held me fast when every instinct of my nature was dragging me away. I am glad now that I had the strength. In spite of all that is has cost me, my manhood is at least above reproach.

Twelve o'clock struck in the distant church, then one, then two. It was the darkest hour of the night. The clouds were drifting low, and there was not a star in the sky. An owl was hooting somewhere among the rocks, but no other sound, save the gentle sough of the wind, came to my ears. And then suddenly I heard it! From far away down the tunnel came those muffled steps, so soft and yet so ponderous. I heard also the rattle of stones as they gave way under that giant tread. They drew nearer. They were close upon me. I heard the crashing of the bushes round the entrance, and then dimly through the darkness I was conscious of the loom of some enormous shape, some monstrous inchoate creature, passing swiftly and very silently out from the tunnel. I was paralysed with fear and amazement. Long as I had waited, now that it had actually come I was unprepared for the shock. I lay motionless and breathless, whilst the great dark mass whisked by me and was swallowed up in the night.

But now I nerved myself for its return. No sound came from the sleeping countryside to tell of the horror which was loose. In no way could I judge how far off it was, what it was doing, or when it might be back. But not a second time should my nerve fail me, not a second time should it pass unchallenged. I swore it between my clenched teeth as I laid my cocked rifle across the rock.

And yet it nearly happened. There was no warning of approach now as the creature passed over the grass. Suddenly, like a dark, drifting shadow, the huge bulk loomed up once more before me, making for the entrance of the cave. Again came that paralysis of volition which held my crooked forefinger impotent upon the trigger. But with a desperate effort I shook it off. Even as the brushwood rustled, and the monstrous beast blended with the shadow of the Gap, I fired at the retreating form. In the blaze of the gun I caught a glimpse of a great shaggy mass, something with rough and bristling hair of a withered grey colour, fading away to white in its lower parts, the huge body supported upon short, thick, curving legs. I had just that glance, and then I heard the rattle of the stones as the creature tore down into its burrow. In an instant, with a triumphant revulsion of feeling, I had cast my fears to the wind, and uncovering my powerful lantern, with my rifle in my hand, I sprang down from my rock and rushed after the monster down the old Roman shaft.

My splendid lamp cast a brilliant flood of vivid light in front of me, very different from the yellow glimmer which had aided me down the same passage only twelve days before. As I ran, I saw the great beast lurching along before me, its huge bulk filling up the whole space from wall to wall. Its hair looked like coarse faded oakum, and hung down in long, dense masses which swayed as it moved. It was like an enormous unclipped sheep in its fleece, but in size it was far larger than the largest elephant, and its breadth seemed to be nearly as great as its height. It fills me with amazement now to think that I should have dared to follow such a horror into the bowels of the earth, but when one's blood is up, and when one's quarry seems to be flying, the old primeval hunting-spirit awakes and prudence is cast to the wind. Rifle in hand, I ran at the top of my speed upon the trail of the monster.

I had seen that the creature was swift. Now I was to find out to my cost that it was also very cunning. I had imagined that it was in panic flight, and that I had only to pursue it. The idea that it might turn upon me never entered my excited brain. I have already explained that the passage down which I was racing opened into a great central cave. Into this I rushed, fearful lest I should lose all trace of the beast. But he had turned upon his own traces, and in a moment we were face to face.

That picture, seen in the brilliant white light of the lantern, is etched for ever upon my brain. He had reared up on his hind legs as a bear would do, and stood above me, enormous, menacing – such a creature as no nightmare had ever brought to my imagination. I have said that he reared like a bear, and there was something bear-like – if one could conceive a bear which was ten-fold the bulk of any bear seen upon earth – in his whole pose and attitude, in his great crooked forelegs with their ivory-white claws, in his rugged skin, and in his red, gaping mouth, fringed with monstrous fangs. Only in one point did he differ from the bear, or from any other creature which walks the earth, and even at that supreme moment a shudder of horror passed over me as I observed that the eyes which glistened in the glow of my lantern were huge, projecting bulbs, white and sightless. For a moment his great paws swung over my head. The next he fell forward upon me, I and my broken lantern crashed to the earth, and I remember no more.

When I came to myself I was back in the farm-house of the Allertons. Two days had passed since my terrible adventure in the Blue John Gap. It seems that I had lain all night in the cave insensible from concussion of the brain, with my left arm and two ribs badly fractured. In the morning my note had been found, a search party of a dozen farmers assembled, and I had been tracked down and carried back to my bedroom, where I had lain in high delirium ever since. There was, it seems, no sign of the creature, and no bloodstain which would show that my bullet had found him as he passed. Save for my own plight and the marks upon the mud, there was nothing to prove that what I said was true.

Six weeks have now elapsed, and I am able to sit out once more in the sunshine. Just opposite me is the steep hillside, grey with shaly rock, and yonder on its flank is the dark cleft which marks the opening of the Blue John Gap. But it is no longer a source of terror. Never again through that ill-omened tunnel shall any strange shape flit out into the world of men. The educated and the scientific, the Dr. Johnsons and the like, may smile at my narrative, but the poorer folk of the countryside had never a doubt as to its truth. On the day after my recovering consciousness they assembled in their hundreds round the Blue John Gap. As the Castleton Courier said:

'It was useless for our correspondent, or for any of the adventurous gentlemen who had come from Matlock, Buxton, and other parts, to offer to descend, to explore the cave to the end, and to finally test the extraordinary narrative of Dr. James Hardcastle. The country people had taken the matter into their own hands, and from an early hour of the morning they had worked hard in stopping up the entrance of the tunnel. There is a sharp slope where the shaft begins, and great boulders, rolled along by many willing hands, were thrust down it until the Gap was absolutely sealed. So ends the episode which has caused such excitement throughout the country. Local opinion is fiercely divided upon the subject. On the one hand are those who point to Dr. Hardcastle's impaired health, and to the possibility of cerebral lesions of tubercular origin giving rise to strange hallucinations. Some *idée fixe**, according to these gentlemen, caused the doctor to wander down the tunnel, and a fall among the rocks was sufficient to account for his injuries. On the other hand, a legend of a strange creature in the Gap has existed for some months back, and the farmers look upon Dr. Hardcastle's narrative and his personal injuries as a final corroboration. So the matter stands, and so the matter will continue to stand, for no definite solution seems to us to be now possible.

* French: fixed idea

It transcends human wit to give any scientific explanation which could cover the alleged facts.' Perhaps before the *Courier* published these words they would have been wise to send their representative to me. I have thought the matter out, as no one else has occasion to do, and it is possible that I might have removed some of the more obvious difficulties of the narrative and brought it one degree nearer to scientific acceptance. Let me then write down the only explanation which seems to me to elucidate what I know to my cost to have been a series of facts. My theory may seem to be wildly improbable, but at least no one can venture to say that it is impossible.

My view is – and it was formed, as is shown by my diary, before my personal adventure – that in this part of England there is a vast subterranean lake or sea, which is fed by the great number of streams which pass down through the limestone. Where there is a large collection of water there must also be some evaporation, mists or rain, and a possibility of vegetation. This in turn suggests that there may be animal life, arising, as the vegetable life would also do, from those seeds and types which had been introduced at an early period of the world's history, when communication with the outer air was more easy. This place had then developed a fauna and flora of its own, including such monsters as the one which I had seen, which may well have been the old cave-bear, enormously enlarged and modified by its new environment. For countless aeons the internal and the external creation had kept apart, growing steadily away from each other. Then there had come some rift in the depths of the mountain which had enabled one creature to wander up and, by means of the Roman tunnel, to reach the open air. Like all subterranean life, it had lost the power of sight, but this had no doubt been compensated for by nature in other directions. Certainly it had some means of finding its way about, and of hunting down the sheep upon the hillside. As to its choice of dark nights, it is part of my theory that light was painful to those great white eyeballs, and that it was only a pitch-black world which it could tolerate. Perhaps, indeed, it was the glare of my lantern which saved my life at that awful moment when we were face to face. So I read the riddle. I leave these facts behind me, and if you can explain them, do so; or if you choose to doubt them, do so. Neither your belief nor your incredulity can alter them, nor affect one whose task is nearly over.

So ended the strange narrative of Dr. James Hardcastle.

Answer key

1 Conversation

Grammar

1

a) Eavesdropping at work can get you into big trouble! / Eavesdropping can get you into big trouble at work!

b) I had a really interesting conversation with a complete stranger recently. / I recently had a really interesting conversation with a complete stranger.

c) I hate people who talk on endlessly about themselves all the time.

d) I overheard the most incredible conversation on the bus the other day! / I overheard the most incredible conversation the other day on the bus!

e) I speak to my grandmother on the phone at least once a month.

f) I tried to phone my boyfriend last night, but he wasn't answering the phone. / Last night I tried to phone my boyfriend, but he wasn't answering the phone.

3

1 Earlier on in the day I had really wanted my parents to meet my boyfriend.

2 She just didn't answer the question frankly.

3 Later I really regretted having asked Jane to come to the party.

4 Normally, I'd just talk to him about it.

5 Jack only knew how to read Arabic.

6 Sometimes I think she finds my obsession with tidiness annoying.

4

1 b
2 b
3 b
4 a
5 b
6 a

5

1 was standing
2 was telling
3 was going
4 was always looking
5 was beginning
6 've bought
7 've remembered
8 'll be getting
9 're watching
10 had been listening
11 hadn't heard
12 were just getting

6

a) ~~been being~~ been
b) ~~have laid~~ be lying
c) ✓
d) ~~might be having~~ might have had
e) ✓
f) ~~been understanding~~ understood
g) ~~he finally gets~~ he's finally getting / he's finally got
h) ✓

Vocabulary

1

a) animated
b) hilarious
c) frustrating
d) in-depth
e) pointless
f) lengthy
g) bizarre
h) one-sided
i) intense; intimate

2

a) put across
b) be on the same wavelength
c) flowed
d) butting in
e) drones on and on
f) hogs
g) hunt around for
h) always has something to say

3

a) butting in
b) hogging
c) flows; hunt around for
d) put … across
e) drones on and on
f) on the same wavelength

4

a) skill
b) efficiently
c) competence
d) fulfil
e) satisfying
f) consideration
g) achievable

5

a) considerate
b) satisfactory
c) fulfilling
d) achievements
e) skilled
f) efficient
g) competent

6

a) Fancy
b) surprise; expecting
c) must; heard
d) got
e) things
f) great

7

1 All good, I hope.
2 Just a sec. Yes, I have. Here you are.
3 Not bad at all. And what about you?
4 Yes, I am, for the first two days. And you?
5 Likewise! I had no idea you knew Lottie.
6 I know, it's totally amazing!

8

a) 4
b) 5
c) 1
d) 2
e) 3
f) 6

Pronunciation

1

a) won't you
b) hasn't he
c) mightn't we
d) haven't you
e) could I
f) will he

2

1. It rises in sentence 1 and falls in sentence 2.
2. a) sentence 2 b) sentence 1

3

a) rising
b) rising
c) falling
d) falling
e) falling
f) rising

Reading

1

a) The Female Brain
b) All Ears
c) Talking from 9 to 5

2

a) C
b) A
c) C
d) B
e) A
f) B
g) C
h) A

3 b

4

a) sardine-style
b) teeming
c) multifarious
d) gets ahead
e) erect
f) stumped
g) accessible

Writing

1

a) F
b) T
c) T
d) T

2

a) show anger
b) using *always* and *never*
c) the argument
d) the other person
e) the problem
f) the opposite of the advice given in the 5 steps

3

1. they
2. that
3. this
4. the

4

Suggested answers
a) scream, shout, sob
b) don't waste time, don't really talk things out
c) how are you going to win the next argument?
d) if you're looking for a bit of peace and quiet, try doing the opposite

5

a) Yes.
b) No.

2 Taste

Grammar

1

We had <u>a great dinner</u>. Lucy cooked for us, she's <u>a fantastic cook</u>. We started with <u>these gorgeous little smoked salmon pancakes</u>. They were absolutely delicious! Then we had <u>some cold cucumber soup</u> and <u>tiny little fingers of crisp toast</u>. <u>The main course</u> was incredible, you really should have seen it. She brought out <u>a tray of fresh lobsters</u> and served them up with <u>a very simple green salad</u>. I thought I couldn't possibly eat any more, but when she brought out the dessert, <u>a home-made chocolate mousse</u>, it was just too good to resist!

2

a) a delicate sweet white wine with just a hint of vanilla
b) a cup of lovely piping hot tea straight from the pot
c) a mixture of tangy citrous juices with just a touch of champagne
d) a glass of ice cold water with a couple of mint leaves and a slice of lemon
e) a glass of fresh full-fat milk straight from the fridge
f) a steaming cup of hot chocolate with a dollop of cream on top

3

a) delicious dark chocolate
b) spicy Mexican bean
c) strong black Italian
d) exquisite hand-painted ceramic
e) large shiny red
f) tiny blue speckled
g) beautiful new china
h) best ice-cold French

5

a) 1 Chelsea's star player Luca Romano went down
  2 The ball went in

b) 1 The days are gone when the boss played God
  2 The name of the game in business today is equality

c) 1 The cathedral stood in the main square
  2 The personal and private worlds of the people who lost their homes, their loved ones and their lives could be glimpsed through the broken facades.

6

a) Down came the rain and washed the dust away.
b) In the kitchen could be heard the sound of raised voices.
c) Bobbing gently on the water were half a dozen fishing boats.
d) The Western Isle was the name of the restaurant.
e) Homely, simple and down-to-earth are the best words to describe it.
f) Long gone were the days of peace and harmony.
g) What had happened, we didn't really know.
h) When she'd be coming back, we had no idea.

Pronunciation

a) cauliflower, criticism
b) cucumber, intricate, microwave, strawberries, vegetables
c) convenience, delicious, exquisite, refreshing, selection

Note: *exquisite* may also be pronounced with the stress on the first syllable.

Vocabulary

1

a) thriving
b) reverie
c) clientele
d) satnav
e) chugged
f) thrust
g) bobbing
h) concrete
i) launch

2

a) ~~informal~~ – homely
b) ~~fantastic~~ – exquisite
c) ~~played loudly~~ – blared out
d) ~~expensive~~ – pricey
e) ~~successful~~ – thriving
f) ~~a mixture of flour, milk and egg whites~~ – batter
g) ~~a businessman~~ – an entrepreneur
h) ~~regular customers~~ – clientele
i) ~~drove away quickly~~ – sped off
j) ~~daydream~~ – reverie

3

a) 4
b) 2
c) 5
d) 1
e) 6
f) 3

4

a) tasteless
b) tasteful
c) taster
d) tasting
e) tasteless
f) tasty
g) tastefully

5

a) bad
b) acquired
c) share
d) accounting
e) medicine
f) victory
g) poor

7

1 That can't be right!
2 That may be, but
3 I know, it's awful, isn't it?
4 that's a load of rubbish!
5 I think you'll find that
6 Oh, I don't know,
7 I rest my case!
8 I suppose you're right.

Listening

1

1 c
2 d
3 a
4 b

2

1 b
2 a
3 d
4 c

3

a) 2
b) 1
c) 4
d) 3

4

a) on
b) to
c) to
d) on
e) on
f) up
g) up
h) at
i) up

Writing

1

a) Spanish
b) friendly and relaxed
c) no

3

a) a film
b) The review gave an inaccurate impression of the film.

4

a) 3
b) 2
c) 1

3 City

Grammar

1

Are mobile phones the new cigarettes?

It has been suggested that cellular phones will be the tobacco of the 21st century. It appears that their use is almost as addictive as cigarettes, with psychologists' reports claiming that there is evidence that users display withdrawal symptoms if deprived of their mobiles for more than 24 hours. There is certainly no doubt that mobile phone use in public is just as annoying as smoking. Mobile-free zones are already being set up in cinemas and restaurants, and it would seem that trains will soon be following suit, with 'mobile' and 'non-mobile' carriages available on all the commuter services to London. On a more serious note, it is now widely believed that excessive mobile phone use may cause cancer, and it has been proposed that all mobile phones should carry a government health warning similar to the one displayed on cigarette packets.

2

a) appears; seems
b) hardly any; little
c) believed; recognised
d) evidence; proof
e) appear; seem
f) proved; shown

3

a) There is no doubt that smoking can lead to cancer.
b) It is widely believed that climate change is the greatest challenge facing our society.
c) It appears that the rate of population growth in China is beginning to decrease.
d) It would seem that people believe governments are not doing enough about global warming.

4

a) no
b) Only
c) no
d) Not
e) Not
f) no
g) Not
h) Only

5

a) after
b) sooner
c) only
d) never
e) after
f) rarely/seldom
g) seldom/rarely/never
h) barely

6

a) Only after I had left the city did I realise how much I loved it.
b) No sooner had we moved into our new cottage than our troubles began.
c) Not only were the local people rude to us, but they also ignored the children.
d) Never had we imagined that people could be so hostile.
e) Only after two months did we make our first friend.
f) Rarely/Seldom did we see him, however, and life was still lonely.
g) Rarely/Seldom/Never had the children been so quiet (before).
h) We decided to go back to the city. Barely had we put up a 'For Sale' sign when the people began to be friendly towards us!

Pronunciation

1

a) Its beauty is not as <u>awe</u>-inspiring as other cities.
b) The streets are lined with s<u>oa</u>ring office blocks.
c) You<u>'re</u> constantly jostled by h<u>aw</u>kers and h<u>or</u>des of tourists.
d) The suburbs haven't f<u>a</u>llen prey to supermarket culture.
e) It's a living city and you'll never run out of things to expl<u>ore</u>.
f) It's the city's hyperactive rush that really dr<u>aws</u> the people here.

2

~~crowded~~ dawn dormitory gawp gorge law ~~modern~~ portray ~~splendour~~ ~~world~~

Vocabulary

1

a) 3
b) 4
c) 5
d) 6
e) 1
f) 2

2

a) magazine
b) meeting
c) family
d) houses
e) chat
f) village

3

a) tacky
b) in-your-face
c) soaring
d) bustling
e) haphazard
f) awe-inspiring

5

a) to make way for a new shopping centre
b) put a finger on
c) lived on top of one another
d) fell prey to
e) worked its magic on me

6

a) buskers 4
b) check out 5
c) gorge 7
d) rant 3
e) gawp at 6
f) handily 1
g) eateries 2

7

1 eateries
2 gorge
3 handily
4 gawp at
5 rant
6 check out
7 buskers

8

a) I really **did enjoy** the film last night. It's one of the best films I've ever seen.
b) You're right about the new stadium. It **does look** a bit out of place.
c) Shopping malls are fine if you're looking for convenience, but I **do think** local street markets are much more interesting.
d) Our neighbours are really friendly, but they **do make** a lot of noise sometimes!
e) My primary school was really small, but it **did have** an enormous playground.
f) My office is a mess. It really **does need** a good, thorough reorganisation.

9

a) The thing I love most about it is the dome.
b) It's the way that it reflects the sunlight that I love.
c) What I also like are the spectacular views from the tower.
d) One thing I don't like is that you have to pay to go inside the cathedral.
e) It's the square with its palm trees swaying in the wind that I love.
f) What I really like is the fact that there's always a cool sea breeze.

Reading

1

The events are now open to women.
The Olympic emblem with the five coloured rings was introduced.
The torch relay was introduced.
The Games are now televised.
The number of events and countries taking part has increased.

2

a) F
b) T
c) F
d) F
e) F
f) F
g) T
h) F

3

a) fierce
b) prestige
c) emblem
d) reinstated
e) tricky
f) cash in on
g) participating
h) in their wake

Writing

1

1 Furthermore,
2 For instance,
3 On the other hand,
4 However,
5 Nonetheless,

2

Suggested answers
 1 ST –
 2 LT +
 3 ST +
 4 ST +
 5 LT +
 6 ST +
 7 ST –
 8 LT +
 9 ST +
10 ST +
11 ST –

4

Suggested answers
a) 4
b) 1
c) 4
d) 4
e) 2
f) 3
g) 2
h) 1

4 Story

Grammar

1

a) of leaving
b) to send
c) to have opened
d) of driving
e) of signing
f) to resume

2

a) were going to leave well before dark
b) was on the verge of giving up hope
c) were hoping / had been hoping to set of by 5.30
d) wasn't going to tell him about Jack
e) was originally to take / to have taken place at nightfall
f) was just about to reveal everything
g) (that) my parents would be a little disappointed
h) was going / had been going to pay her a visit

3

1 would be swallowing
2 would be living
3 were on the verge of colonising
4 were going to be delivering
5 would be
6 were going to be flying
7 would last

5

a) 2
b) 1
c) 8
d) 5
e) 4
f) 7
g) 6
h) 3

6

a) particularly
b) Likewise
c) such as; too
d) To be accurate
e) Strictly speaking
f) or even
g) that is to say; on the other hand
h) In addition
i) at any rate
j) then
k) Say

Vocabulary

1

a) short story
b) fairy tale
c) fable
d) legend
e) whodunnit
f) anecdote
g) myth(s)
h) news story

3

a) End of story
b) it's a long story
c) tell tales
d) cock and bull story
e) the story of my life
f) sob story
g) to cut a long story short
h) old wives' tale

4

a) unfaithful
b) astute
c) gullible
d) plausible
e) unscrupulous
f) sceptical
g) fishy

5

1 f
2 c
3 g
4 e
5 d
6 b
7 a

6

a) 4
b) 6
c) 7
d) 8
e) 2
f) 3
g) 5
h) 1

7

a) How awful / What a nightmare / Oh no
b) I don't blame you / I'm not surprised / Quite right
c) What a nightmare / Oh no / How awful
d) Lucky you
e) What a relief

Pronunciation

1

a) ✓
b) ✗

2

a) i) ✗   ii) ✓
b) i) ✗   ii) ✓
c) i) ✓   ii) ✗
d) i) ✓   ii) ✗
e) i) ✗   ii) ✓
f) i) ✓   ii) ✗

Listening

1

a) Della and Jim
b) They are married.
c) Della – her beautiful hair; Jim – his gold pocket watch
d) hair combs, a gold chain for the watch

2

a) 3
b) 9
c) 1
d) 2
e) 4
f) 5
g) 8
h) 6
i) 7

No, the events happened in a different order. The selling of the watch is delayed until the very end so that we discover the irony of the Christmas presents at the same time as Della.

3

a) scrape together
b) auburn
c) flung on
d) marched
e) lock
f) prized
g) handed over
h) glimpse
i) trembling
j) fumbled

Writing

1

The following are included:
a, b, d, e, f, i, j

2

a) 9
b) 11
c) 8
d) 10
e) 5
f) 1
g) 2
h) 7
i) 6
j) 12
k) 3/4
l) 4/3

5 Bargain

Grammar

1

Flower power
A florist's in Coventry is offering bunches of dead roses wrapped in black paper for jilted lovers to send to their ex-partners. The owner says the inspiration for the idea was her partner, <u>whom she split up with last month</u>.

Security risk
A shoplifter was yesterday given a six-week jail sentence by a court in Rotherham after he removed a security tag from an item of clothing and tried to walk out of the shop with it so it couldn't be used as evidence. "It's not something <u>I'm proud of,</u>" Paul Wood, 26, said as he left the court. It is the fifth shoplifting offence <u>of which Wood has been convicted</u>.

Counting on the money
A woman from Dewsbury, <u>for whom Dracula and vampires have been a life-long obsession</u>, has set up a company which imports and sells coffins from Transylvania. The company sells five different products, <u>the most popular of which is painted blood red</u>.

Hitting the jackpot
A man <u>for whom the local golf club was a second home</u> and who took his wife to bingo only to stop her complaining has won the £200,000 jackpot at a club in Bristol. And what is the lucky Mr Jones going to treat himself to first? "There's a new set of clubs <u>I've been saving up for,</u>" he said.

2

a) This is the shop I got my camera from.
b) Is this the hotel ~~which~~ we stayed in last year?
c) Jo is someone on whom you can always rely.
d) It's technically a crime, but nothing for which you'd be arrested.
e) The person ~~who~~ you need to speak to is not here at the moment.
f) Are they the people with whom Luke went on holiday?

3

a) This is the shop from which I got my camera.   F
   This is the shop I got my camera from.   I
b) Is this the hotel in which we stayed last year?   F
   Is this the hotel ~~which~~ we stayed in last year?   I
c) Jo is someone you can always rely on.   I
   Jo is someone on whom you can always rely.   F
d) It's technically a crime, but nothing you'd be arrested for.   I
   It's technically a crime, but nothing for which you'd be arrested.   F
e) The person to whom you need to speak is not here at the moment.   F
   The person ~~who~~ you need to speak to is not here at the moment.   I
f) Are they the people Luke went on holiday with?   I
   Are they the people with whom Luke went on holiday?   F

4

a) He earns about $200 a week, most of which he spends on computer games.
b) I've got a few friends in the UK, most of whom live in London.
c) We made loads of food for the party, most of which didn't get eaten.
d) There are about forty university colleges in Oxford, the oldest of which is Balliol College.
e) We've got exams all next week, the first of which is maths.

5

a) In 2003, – Manchester United bought Portuguese footballer Cristiano Ronaldo as **a** replacement for David Beckham. **The** club paid £12 million for Ronaldo. In – June 2009, Ronaldo was sold to – Real Madrid for £80 million, giving the club **a** profit of £68 million on – top of **the** three league titles and six trophies they won while he was playing for them.

b) Swiss watches and **the** companies making them used to be **the** envy of **the** world. However, primarily due to strong competition from – Japanese companies during **the** 1970s and 80s, sales of – Swiss watches worldwide fell drastically. **The** Swiss and **the** Japanese decided to collaborate and the result was **a** product called 'Swatch'. Today 'Swatch' accounts for – 50% of all – watches sold.

c) In **the** early 1950s, smalltime record producer Sam Phillips had **an** exclusive contract with **a** young unknown singer he had discovered. In 1955, he sold **the** contract to **the** RCA record company for – $35,000. That singer was Elvis Presley and Phillips lost –/**the** income from over **a** billion records, CDs and downloads.

d) In 1888, businessman Asa Chandler bought **the** rights to – Coca-Cola from its inventor, John Pemberton. This is generally regarded as one of **the** best business decisions ever made. However, ten years later, in one of **the** worst business decisions ever, Chandler sold **the** bottling rights for just $1. Today, **a** billion units of Coca-Cola are produced each day.

e) In one of **the** most infamous business decisions ever made, Decca Records turned down **the** Beatles in – January 1962. After **a** 15-song audition at Decca studios, **the** company told **the** group's manager, Brian Epstein, 'We don't like your boys' sound. – Groups are out; four-piece groups with – guitars particularly are finished.'

6

a) office; shops
b) home; school
c) work; school
d) Tom's house; Café Coco
e) café; cinema
f) police; government
g) music of Brahms; Brahms you were playing last night
h) university; school
i) paella in this restaurant; paella my mother makes

8

a) the –
b) – a
c) – a
d) – the
e) the –
f) a –
g) the –

Pronunciation

a) /ðə/ TV remote control is on /ðə/ table.
b) Is /ði/umbrella in /ðə/ hall?
c) This is /ði/ oldest building in /ðə/ city.
d) Don't use /ðə/ printer. /ði/ ink's running out.
e) /ði/ ice-rink is next to /ðə/ park. Just before /ðə/ university.
f) /ði/ exam's on /ði/ 8th. In /ði/ afternoon.
g) /ðə/ film was great. /ðə/ scene at /ði/ end was amazing.

Vocabulary

1

a) make do
b) shop around
c) impulse buy
d) slap-up meal
e) down-payment

3

1 get into
2 live on
3 run up
4 splashing out
5 get by
6 save up
7 cutting back
8 get around
9 came in
10 paying off

a) 2
b) 5
c) 6
d) 4
e) 9
f) 7
g) 8
h) 3
i) 10
j) 1

4

a) the red
b) cost; frills
c) off; robbery

5

a) broke
b) discounted
c) lavish
d) affordable
e) overpriced
f) exorbitant
g) frugal

6

a) that's a bit more than I was prepared to pay
b) Could you give me a discount
c) it's still a bit above my price range
d) Is that your best price
e) I think I'll leave it then
f) how much do you want to pay
g) Right, I'll take it

Reading

1

Kyle MacDonald traded a paper clip for a house via several other trades including a fish-shaped pen, a snow globe and a Hollywood film role.

2

a) He was living in rented accommodation with his girlfriend.
b) He was a pizza delivery man and couldn't afford to buy his own house.
c) To set up a website and trade a red paperclip for something bigger and better and to trade that item and so on until he had a house.
d) He got the idea from the children's game 'Bigger and Better'.
e) Because at one point he traded an afternoon with rock star Alice Cooper for a snow globe.
f) One of the inhabitants of Kipling.
g) The level of interest from the public.
h) Make a wedding ring out of it.

3

swap   exchanged

4

a) set out to
b) goal
c) out of the question
d) set up
e) lost the plot
f) string
g) novel
h) quirky
i) stirred up
j) housewarming party

Writing

1

a) 6
b) 4
c) 5
d) 1
e) 2
f) 3

2

a) The story is about a man who sold his 'entire life' on eBay because he had recently split up with his wife and he wanted to make a fresh start.
b) iii
c) Ian Usher's feelings about the sale 6
The idea and why it came about 3
A brief summary of the story 1
The events of the actual sale 5
Ian Usher's plans for the future 7
Details about what was for sale 4
Background information about Ian Usher 2

6 Mind

Grammar

1

a) I'm feeling – I feel
b) ✓
c) been hearing – listened to / been listening to
d) was hearing – heard / could hear
e) ✓
f) I'm smelling – I can smell
g) ✓
h) is tasting – tastes

2

a) can hear
b) couldn't taste
c) 'm smelling
d) able to hear
e) *both are possible*
f) could smell
g) can feel
h) *both are possible*

3

a) listening
b) can hear
c) taste / smell
d) can feel
e) 'm feeling / feel
f) could see
g) smell
h) looking
i) watch
j) feel

4

1 having spent
2 hearing
3 demanding
4 having overbooked
5 shouting and protesting
6 wanting
7 Appeased

5

a) Not having understood what she'd said, he did the exercise incorrectly.
b) Being English, he finds it hard to follow them when they start speaking Czech.
c) Having worked really hard at the meeting, we all went out for a meal on the company.
d) Not knowing the area very well, there's a danger he'll get lost.
e) Cleared / Having been cleared of theft by the courts, he immediately got his old job back.
f) Lost in thought, he didn't notice that his train had pulled out of the station.
g) Not being particularly interested in the talk, she decided not to go.
h) Delayed by the traffic on the motorway, James was extremely late.
i) Intrigued by the news, she wanted to know more.
j) Not having made a very good impression at the interview, she was worried that she wouldn't get the job.

Vocabulary

1

a) gaze
b) examine
c) recognise
d) dart
e) observe
f) scan

2

a) examined
b) darting
c) recognise
d) observed
e) scanned
f) gazed

3

a) admit – recognise
b) understand – see
c) wrote – observed
d) acknowledged – recognised
e) remarked – observed
f) meeting – seeing
g) follow – observe
h) realised – recognised

4

a) phobia
b) overcome
c) nap
d) docile
e) addiction
f) tattered
g) spotted

5

a) how
b) own
c) two
d) off
e) out
f) alike
g) over
h) on

6

a) the last thing on my mind
b) mind her own business
c) in two minds
d) mind over matter
e) Mind how you go
f) great minds think alike
g) going out of my mind
h) take your mind off

7

a) Is it OK if I leave this until tomorrow?
b) Would you mind repeating that, please?
c) May I bring my husband with me?
d) Do you mind if I smoke at the table?
e) Would you mind awfully turning the volume down a little / turning down the volume a little?
f) Can I swap seats with you, please?

8

a) 2
b) 4
c) 6
d) 5
e) 3
f) 1

Pronunciation

1

a) stimulation
b) observation
c) recognition
d) action/activity
e) regularity
f) creation/creativity
g) popularity
h) perfection
i) familiarity
j) anxiety

2

a) s<u>ti</u>mulate, stimul<u>a</u>tion
b) obs<u>er</u>ve, obser<u>va</u>tion
c) r<u>e</u>cognise, recog<u>ni</u>tion
d) <u>a</u>ctive, <u>a</u>ction, ac<u>ti</u>vity
e) r<u>e</u>gular, regul<u>a</u>rity
f) cr<u>e</u>ative, cre<u>a</u>tion, crea<u>ti</u>vity
g) <u>po</u>pular, popul<u>a</u>rity
h) p<u>er</u>fect, per<u>fec</u>tion
i) fa<u>mi</u>liar, famili<u>a</u>rity
j) <u>an</u>xious, an<u>xi</u>ety

Listening

1

a) Mark: work
   Kay: commuting to work
   Liz: looking after her children
b) Mark: he finds it hard to relax after work
   Kay: she feels tired at the end of the day and often suffers from headaches
   Liz: sometimes she gets so tired she cries
c) *Any two of the following:*
   Mark: does sport, goes running, goes to the gym, plays squash
   Kay: has a hot bath, plays some soft music, reads a book, does some cooking
   Liz: leaves the children with their grandmother, goes to a film or art exhibition, reads the newspaper, meets a friend for lunch

2

a) Liz
b) Kay
c) Mark and Kay
d) Mark
e) Mark
f) Liz
g) Liz
h) Kay

3

a) unwind
b) fidgety
c) get away
d) pent-up
e) soul-destroying
f) drained
g) curl up
h) turning to pulp

Writing

1

Fran must have complained about problems at work, probably that she was being overworked and that she was thinking of giving up her job.

2

Dear Fran,

How are you? You sounded really low in your last letter. Are things getting any better? Were you serious about resigning or were you just going through a bad patch? Look, if the job's really that bad, I think you should give it up. Nothing's worth getting that stressed out about. But if you're really determined to stick it out – and I know you, you can be really stubborn sometimes – you should really try looking after yourself a bit better. I'm sure you can find ways to delegate some of your work or to cut down your workload. They really are asking too much of you.

I think the best thing you could do would be to sit down with your boss and talk about the situation. Maybe she doesn't realise the pressure you're under. Or maybe you could try asking for a short holiday before you literally work yourself into the ground. You can't keep working the way you have been, it'll make you ill.

Right, sorry, I sound like your mother! But seriously, if there's anything I can do, please let me know. Whatever you decide to do, I'm sure you'll make the right decision and it'll all work out fine in the long run. In the meantime, phone me. I'd love to hear from you and maybe we can make some plans to meet up. Take care and don't let it get you down.

A huge hug and lots of love,
Steve

3

I think you should
you should really try
I think the best thing you could do would be to
maybe you could try

4

a) final exams
b) she can't sleep and she's getting irritable
c) to try to take time out from studying in order to relax

7 Digital

Grammar

1

1 light
2 business people who
3 and home
4 for a small
5 can carry
6 have to carry
7 don't want
8 Speech recognition
9 navigate your computer
10 write documents
11 you could
12 keyboard and mouse

2

Netbooks ~~are~~ inexpensive and light ~~They~~ appeal to a wide audience. ~~They appeal~~ to business people who travel frequently. ~~They appeal~~ to kids and home users. ~~They are~~ looking for a small laptop. ~~They want to be able to~~ carry it from room to room. ~~They also appeal~~ to students. ~~They~~ have to carry heavy books around ~~with them~~ all day. ~~They~~ don't want the extra weight of a full size laptop.

Speech recognition has reached ~~an important~~ point ~~in its development. With speech recognition~~ you can navigate your computer ~~without a keyboard and mouse.~~ ~~You can also~~ write documents without ~~using~~ the keyboard and mouse. ~~It's much~~ faster ~~with speech recognition.~~

3

a) The perfect computer would be one that is so small and light it can fit comfortably in your pocket, but at the same time can open out to give you a full size screen.
b) I think speech recognition could do so many good things , such as help people with physical disabilities to access all the functions on their computer quickly and easily.
c) I would love to have a car that can park itself, lining itself up in the parking space and doing all that awkward manoeuvring for me!

5

1 S
2 D
3 D
4 D
5 S

Possible answers
2b We'll definitely see someone we know at the party.
3b He might not be of the same opinion tomorrow …
4b Experts believe that the present generation of children will probably …

6

a) Sea levels are likely **to** rise by over a metre by the end of the 21st century.
b) There **may well** be more electric cars than traditional petrol fuelled cars on our roads in as little as five years.
c) ✓
d) With new advances in nanotechnology, cancer and tumours will **almost certainly** become a thing of the past.
e) ✓
f) Scientists are bound to discover~~ing~~ a cure for Alzheimer's disease by the end of the century.
g) Human beings **definitely won't** ever be able to live to more than 120.
h) ✓

Vocabulary

1

a) central heating
b) keypad
c) keyboard
d) earpiece
e) touchscreen
f) evening meal
g) card reader
h) remote control
i) wristband
j) voicemail

2

a) device
b) coverage
c) network
d) scheme
e) alert
f) voicemail
g) entertainment
h) shopping
i) recognition

3

a) wowed
b) trashed
c) went digital
d) slick
e) sold on the idea
f) hype

4

1 hype
2 wowed
3 slick
4 sold on the idea
5 go digital
6 trashed

5

a) deal
b) through
c) back
d) done; done
e) possible
f) round; round
g) sleep
h) end

Pronunciation

a) phone
b) control
c) travel
d) heating
e) touch
f) wrist

Reading

1

a) invisibility cloak
b) surgeons / see the patients they are operating on
c) airline pilots / land safely
d) a wall / a camera / watch what's happening outside

2

a) the invisibility cloak
b) it makes the object under it seem transparent
c) heat haze or a mirage in the desert
d) virtual invisibility or optical camouflage
e) Japan 2003
f) surveillance / using the technology to watch people without being observed
g) future legal and security implications

3

a) unveiled
b) shields
c) fuzziness
d) mirage
e) optical illusion
f) hey presto!
g) outlaw

Writing

1

a, d, h

2 c

3

Paragraph **b** is the best. Paragraph **a** goes into too much detail too soon

4

1 Not only
2 it also meant that
3 Prior to
4 But with
5 For the first time

8 Law

Grammar

1

a) In her kitchen, listening to the radio, Katie heard that the radio station was giving away free sports cars.
b) What you had to do to win a sports car was answer three simple questions.
c) Putting down the potatoes she was peeling, Katie phoned the radio station.
d) The three questions were read out (by the DJ) and Katie answered them correctly.
e) What the DJ did when she went to the radio station to collect her prize, was hand her a 10cm model of a sports car.
f) Furious, Katie decided to sue the radio station.
g) Ruling in her favour, the court ordered the radio station to pay Katie £40,000 for the real car.

2

1 would
2 must
3 should / ought to
4 would/could
5 might/could/may
6 'd/would
7 ought

3

a) She promised she **would** phone if there were any problems.
b) I'm really sorry, I **should** have been looking where I was going.
c) I know I really ought **to** have phoned sooner, but I was terribly busy.
d) His phone was engaged. I suppose he might have **been** talking to his sister.
e) I thought he'd have arrived by now; he must **have** got stuck in the traffic.
f) Why's the light still on? You should **have** been asleep by now!
g) You should have told me there was no food in the house – I **would** have gone to the shops.
h) I'm sorry, I really don't know where it is – I suppose I might have left it at home.

4

a) He's over an hour late. He must have forgotten about the appointment.
b) He explained that he couldn't afford to buy a new car because it was far too expensive.
c) She believes it might have been intentional.
d) You should have got the boiler checked …
e) Cathy promised she would make sure all the doors were locked and all the lights switched off.
f) They couldn't have stolen the money, they didn't have enough time.
g) He can't have known about your news, or he'd have said something.
h) You could have let us know you were coming to town last weekend.
i) I really don't know what I did with my sunglasses. I may have left them at the restaurant.
j) Cara used to be a terrible time-keeper when she was younger. She would always turn up late for everything.

5

a) 6
b) 5
c) 2
d) 7
e) 1
f) 4
g) 3

6

a) So disappointed was he with the outcome of the court case that he decided to give up practising law.
b) She wasn't expecting to get the job, nor did she expect to be offered such a generous salary.
c) He hates the fact that he has to work on the night shift and so does his wife, who has to spend the evenings alone.
d) Such was the confusion over the new voting system, that many people voted for the wrong candidate.
e) So bad is his reputation for not paying his debts that no one will lend him any money.
f) She was neither happy to help nor (was she) willing to say why.
g) Such was their surprise when he told them (that) he'd passed his exam, that they could hardly believe him.

Vocabulary

1

a) 2
b) 1
c) 2
d) 3
e) 2
f) 3

2

a) sue
b) arson
c) The accused
d) community service
e) cross examine
f) return a verdict
g) speeding
h) libel

3

a) unto
b) down
c) into
d) above
e) with
f) is
g) by
h) against

4

a) taking the law into your own hands
b) in trouble with the law
c) lay down the law
d) above the law
e) a law unto himself
f) by law
g) against the law
h) word is law

5

a) 4
b) 5
c) 7
d) 2
e) 3
f) 8
g) 1
h) 6

6

1 prominent; seeking
2 commence; severe
3 depicting; prior to
4 Further; in due course

7

a) hear
b) got
c) expect
d) never; thought
e) tell
f) can't
g) kidding
h) believe

8

a) And pigs might fly!
b) You can't judge a book by its cover.
c) Still waters run deep.
d) Pull the other one.

9

1 c
2 d
3 b
4 a

Listening

1

a) Employers do not have to pay their employees when they're on jury service.
b) You can learn about how the justice system works.

2

a) T
b) F
c) F
d) F
e) F
f) T
g) T
h) F

3

a) out
b) off
c) on
d) at
e) in
f) out
g) at
h) on
i) from

Writing

1 a

2

1 Figures
2 Over a quarter
3 more likely
4 compared with
5 than by those
6 was found
7 the vast majority
8 an average

3

a) 60%
b) 52%
c) burglaries
d) muggings
e) job
f) 40%
g) stable employment

9 Night

Grammar

1

a) however
b) though
c) but
d) although
e) even though
f) however
g) Despite
h) yet

2

1 even though
2 though
3 despite
4 but
5 However
6 Even though
7 yet
8 Despite
9 nevertheless
10 However
11 despite
12 Try as I might
13 but
14 That said

4

a) I'd worked harder.
b) I hadn't stolen that car.
c) I'd gone to bed earlier.
d) not going to the hairdresser.
e) I'd booked in advance.

5

a) I really wish I hadn't drunk so much.
b) I really regret eating / having eaten so much.
c) I wish I hadn't danced with Anna!
d) If only I'd got to speak / spoken to Katie.
e) I so wish I hadn't sung 'I will survive' at karaoke!
f) I so regret making a fool of myself.

6

a) not having had
b) had invented
c) had known; would have taken
d) had had; would have been
e) wouldn't have lived; was going

Pronunciation

1

a) *had* is pronounced as /d/
b) *had* is pronounced as /d/; *would* is pronounced as /d/; *have* is pronounced as /əv/

2

a) If only I'**d** gone out last night.
b) I wish I'**d** had more time.
c) If you'**d** been there, you'**d've** loved it.
d) I'**d** like to'**ve** gone with you.
e) Peter'**d've** loved it too.

Vocabulary

1

```
N D S U N S E T F
M I D N I G H T M
D B G K N R T J I
A U Y H S O Q L D
W Z S H T P O H D
N B X K Q F M N A
D A Y B R E A K Y
S U N R I S E L V
T W I L I G H T L
```

sunset   dawn
midnight   midday
daybreak   nightfall
sunrise   dusk
twilight   noon

2

a) the middle of the night
b) the wee small hours
c) first thing in the morning
d) last thing at night
e) the crack of dawn
f) mid-afternoon

3

a) the middle of the night
b) the crack of dawn
c) mid-afternoon
d) the wee small hours
e) last thing at night
f) first thing in the morning

4

a) hen night
b) stag night
c) nightlife
d) overnight
e) night on the town
f) all night long
g) nightcap
h) early night

5

a) off
b) down
c) alert
d) log
e) light
f) wink
g) light
h) batteries

6

1 b
2 a
3 d
4 c
5 f
6 e
7 h
8 g

7

a) No, what did you have in mind?
b) What are you up to this evening?
c) I was wondering if you'd like to go for a drink sometime?
d) That's really kind of you, but I'm going out tonight.
e) I'm afraid I've got something on then.
f) I can't make Friday, but I'm free on Saturday.

8

1 up
2 eyes
3 shame
4 fancied
5 up
6 time
7 mind
8 sometime
9 sounds
10 about
11 good
12 could
13 make
14 Say
15 along
16 fancies
17 then
18 to

Reading

1

c) and d) are not mentioned

2

a) T
b) F
c) T
d) F
e) T
f) T
g) F
h) T

3

a) disruptive
b) deprivation
c) consensus
d) take stock
e) recuperate
f) down time
g) stunted
h) susceptibility
i) prosaic
j) disputed

4

d)

Writing

1

a)
Summary of research to date 2
What experts agree on 4
Background 1
The theories 3

b) Studies have shown that growth in children can be stunted by sleep deprivation and in adults, insufficient sleep increases susceptibility to disease.
c) view   explanation
d) yet (para 1) despite (para 1) However (para 5) while (para 5) While (para 6)

2

a) yet
b) Despite
c) One theory
d) Another theory
e) However
f) While

10 Footprints

Grammar

1

1 is given
2 were changed
3 is believed
4 were created
5 is known
6 are owned
7 were stolen
8 have yet to be / are yet to be
9 were sold
10 were inspired
11 were recently put / have recently been put
12 were / are weaved / woven
13 (are) set
14 had been taken / were taken
15 were placed
16 (were / are) guarded

2

a) The world's most expensive shoes were made by American designer Stuart Weitzman.
b) The shoes are valued at $3 million.
c) The shoes are currently owned by Princess Yasmin Aga Khan, the daughter of legendary actress Rita Hayworth.
d) The shoes' centrepiece is a pair of earrings once worn / that had once been worn by the actress.
e) The shoes were worn by Kathleen York, a nominee at the Oscars in 2006.
f) There is now a pair of Weitzman shoes every year at the Oscars and there is always great excitement about who they will be worn by.
g) Several other pairs of Weitzman's shoes have been sold for over $1 million.

3

1 ever taken
2 was made
3 photographed
4 was found
5 will not be disturbed
6 is eventually eroded
7 have been made/left
8 left/made
9 having been given
10 spoken
11 is finally being discussed
12 is predicted

4

a) by far
b) very slightly
c) just
d) somewhat
e) considerably
f) nothing like

Vocabulary

1

a) locally-grown
b) renewable
c) solar-powered
d) organic
e) energy-efficient
f) Sustainable
g) recycled

2

a) 2
b) 1
c) 3
d) 4
e) 5/8
f) 9
g) 6
h) 5/8
i) 7

3

a) I put my foot in it.
b) I've got itchy feet.
c) I've got a foot in the door.
d) I waited on him hand and foot.
e) I put my foot down.
f) I need to stand on my own two feet.
g) I got cold feet.
h) I put my feet up.
i) I didn't put a foot wrong.

4

5

a) go
b) defeatist
c) go
d) do   good
e) know   want
f) twisted   arm
g) happy
h) point
i) ventured   gained

6

a) What's the point of buying a piano if you're not going to learn to play it?
b) What's the point of having a well-paid job if you never spend anything?
c) What's the point of going on holiday if you're always phoning the office?
d) What's the point of joining a gym if you never go?
e) What's the point of getting a new mobile if there's nothing wrong with your old one?

Pronunciation

1

a) Russia is <u>far</u> bigger than China.
b) The book is <u>way</u> better than the film.

2

a) Computer games are <u>way</u> better than they used to be.
b) The film is nowhere <u>near</u> as good as the book.
c) Canada is only <u>slightly</u> bigger than the USA.
d) Soccer is nothing <u>like</u> as popular as baseball.
e) The bus is only a <u>bit</u> cheaper than the train.
f) Computers are <u>infinitely</u> more user-friendly these days.

Listening

1

a) 3
b) 4
c) 5
d) 1
e) 2

2

a) 1
b) 1
c) 3
d) 2
e) 3
f) helpful   welcoming   relaxed   friendly

3

Leave a minimum of impact on the places you visit.

4

a) hustle and bustle – lively activity
b) a happening place – a place with a lot of things happening
c) a well-trodden path – a route that many people take
d) worth checking out – worth going to see or experience
e) soak up the atmosphere – experience and enjoy the atmosphere
f) watch the world go by – watch daily life happening

Writing

2

She wants some recommendations for visiting Nepal.

3

He recommends a, b, f and h.

4

a) worth
b) see
c) to
d) get
e) interested
f) Whatever
g) get
h) sure
i) tempted
j) have
k) change

11 Words

Grammar

1

1 f
2 f
3 d
4 a
5 a
6 c
7 d
8 d
9 c
10 i
11 b
12 h

2

Suggested answers

A: It's Tom's 30th ~~birthday party~~ tonight. Are you going ~~to the party~~? ~~If you're going to the party~~ **If so**, I can give you a lift.
B: ~~Where is the party taking place?~~ **Where is it?**
A: ~~The party's taking place~~ at his brother's bar, I think.
B: Nobody told me anything about ~~the party~~ **it**. Maybe I haven't been invited ~~to go to the party~~. Are you going?
A: Yes. Tom invited me ~~to the party~~ last week when I saw ~~Tom~~ **him** at the golf club. We were ~~both at the golf club~~ **there** with our bosses. ~~Our bosses~~ **They** play golf together every Thursday.
B: I didn't know ~~your boss played with Tom's boss~~ **that**. How long have they been ~~playing golf together every week~~ doing that?
A: ~~They've been playing together~~ for as long as I can remember. Anyway, going back to Tom's party, you should definitely come. I'm sure Tom will be disappointed if you don't ~~come to his party~~. I'll see you ~~at Tom's party~~ **there**.

Pronunciation

A: ~~Are~~ you ready to go out?
B: No, not yet, ~~I'm~~ just finishing this bit of work.
A: OK, ~~we'll~~ meet you there, then.
B: Yeah, ~~I'll~~ be there in about half an hour.
A: OK. ~~We'll~~ catch you later!

A: ~~Did~~ you see John last night?
B: No, was he supposed to be there then?
A: ~~As~~ far as I know, yes.
B: Hm. ~~He~~ must have got caught up at work or something.
A: ~~I~~ suppose so.

Vocabulary

1

a) always connected
b) conspicuous consumerism
c) credit crunch
d) digital down time
e) face time
f) lipstick economy

2

a) always connected
b) lipstick economy
c) credit crunch
d) conspicuous consumerism
e) digital down time
f) face time

3

a) **right**sizing
b) **up**skill
c) phone**ography**
d) Net**speak**
e) **life**casting
f) **recession**ista

4

a) glean
b) favour
c) tangents
d) rambling
e) going around the houses
f) put himself across
g) hit the right note
h) sank in

5

1 words
2 point
3 saying
4 what
5 that

Reading

1 b

2

1 c
2 a
3 b
4 e
5 d

3

a) jeopardise
b) erroneous
c) tailor
d) convey
e) pledge
f) pertains
g) disconcerting
h) typo

Writing

1

a) ✗
b) ✗
c) ✓
d) ✗
e) ✓
f) ✓
g) ✗
h) ✓
i) ✗
j) ✗
k) ✓
l) ✓

2

a) freelance translator
b) a, b, c, d, e, g, i, j

3

apply
European
trainee
went
currently
permanent
skills
from
experience
interview

4

a) I'm writing to …
b) I am currently looking for …
c) I think your company will benefit from …
d) I am available for interview …

12 Conscience

Grammar

1

a) 4
b) 3
c) 7
d) 5
e) 1
f) 2
g) 6

2

a) join – joined
b) spent – spend
c) don't – didn't
d) wouldn't be – weren't/wasn't
e) can – could
f) not do – didn't do
g) would do – did
h) might give – gave

3

a) It's high time the local authorities did something about the traffic.
b) I'd rather you didn't smoke in my car.
c) It's high time someone taught him a few manners. He's very rude.
d) It's about time he stopped wasting time and settled down to a good job.
e) I'd rather you stayed at home and looked after the children so that I can/could go shopping.

Pronunciation

1

a) bungee
b) sister
c) fun
d) thinking

The stress falls on those words because the responses are correcting a misunderstanding in the first sentence.

2

a) Relief
b) clothes
c) brother
d) school

Vocabulary

1

a) wino – 2
b) beggars – 3
c) street person – 1

2

a) reunited
b) secure
c) addressing
d) pursue
e) represent
f) boost

3

a) a clear
b) on her
c) In all
d) ease my
e) an easy
f) a guilty

4

a) I'm really sorry. It won't happen again.
b) I think I owe you an apology.
c) Sorry, I had no idea this was your seat.
d) I'm sorry, it totally slipped my mind.
e) I really am terribly sorry. I had no idea.
f) We regret to inform you that all trains have been cancelled due to bad weather.

5

1 f
2 a
3 c
4 b
5 e
6 d

Listening

1

a) 1985
b) to raise funds for victims of a famine in Sudan and Ethiopia
c) it was first set up by comedians (and it uses comedy and laughter to get its message across)
d) Red Nose Day
e) Red Nose Fun Run, Red Dinner Party, role-reversal events

2 d, f

3

a) devastating
b) refugee
c) good
d) catchy
e) role
f) organised
g) silly

Writing

1

1 c
2 d
3 a
4 b

2

1 d
2 a
3 b
4 c

3

b) *For example:*
speaking directly to the reader: *Here's what you have to do.*
using questions: *What's it all about?*
using exclamations: *Now's your chance!*
using adjectives: *outrageous, unbelievable headgear; fantastic, fun-filled fancy dress festival*

4

1 a
2 a
3 b
4 b